Bill Moore

BARACK OBAMA

WORDS THAT INSPIRED A NATION

William W. Moore
659 Paw Paw Creek Rd.
Fairview, WV 26570-9350

D1450179

BARACK OBAMA

WORDS THAT INSPIRED A NATION

ESSENTIAL SPEECHES: 2002 TO THE INAUGURATION

Foreword by Victor Dorff

FALL RIVER PRESS

Fall River Press
122 Fifth Avenue
New York, NY 10011

ISBN: 978-1-4351-1769-3

Printed and bound in the United States of America

1 3 5 7 9 10 8 6 4 2

"It was the call of workers who organized; women who reached for the ballot; a president who chose the moon as our new frontier; and a King who took us to the mountaintop and pointed the way to the Promised Land. Yes we can, to justice and equality. Yes we can, to opportunity and prosperity. Yes we can heal this nation. Yes we can repair this world."

Contents

Foreword

The presidential election of November 2008 is, without a doubt, a moment in history that will be studied by generations to come. Surely our children's children will see a drama nuanced with meanings and implications we cannot even imagine. Because Barack Obama is truly an orator, however, the kernel of his story can be found in the speeches he gave along the way to becoming the first African-American president of the United States.

With the now-iconic phrases, "Yes we can," "Choose hope over fear," and "Our moment is now," Obama delivered an uplifting message of unity, change, responsibility, and faith. His speeches were sometimes soaring and profound, sometimes quietly poetic, but always unflinchingly realistic about the difficulties the country faced and the sacrifices required to overcome them. Their content and their cadence conveyed the vision of the man, his ability to inspire, his understanding of historical context, and his focus on the future.

Speeches are meant to be heard, like music. But just as the lyrics of some songs stand alone as poetry, the words of some orators are so completely infused with ideas that, to be truly *heard*, they must be *read*—again and again. Most of the orators who delivered such pithy and resonant speeches are of a time long past, but Barack Obama has shown that the power of rhetoric is still a mighty force in American politics.

The collection of speeches you hold in your hands embodies the incredible sense of momentum generated by the man who captured the imagination of a nation by articulating, with clarity and grace, a message that America was finally ready to hear.

Challenging the Call to War

One year after the terrorist attacks of September 11, 2001, as President George W. Bush made the case for war in Iraq, Democrats were sharply divided.

Many were afraid of appearing weak in the face of danger or being labeled "unpatriotic."

With that as a backdrop, Barack Obama's 2002 address to an antiwar rally in Chicago set him apart. Repeating that he was "not opposed to war in all circumstances," he carefully established his *willingness* to fight, but only when necessary and appropriate. Largely unknown, this state senator skillfully used the form of a question to issue a challenge, in colloquial terms, to the most powerful man on earth: "You want a fight, President Bush?" Obama called on the sitting president to refocus his attention on issues he deemed more worthy of battle, such as defeating Al Qaeda, preventing the proliferation of nuclear weapons, and ending America's dependence on foreign oil. A few days later, less than one month before the 2002 midterm elections, the U.S. Congress voted overwhelmingly to authorize an attack on Iraq.

Obama Bursts onto the National Scene

Two years later, Barack Obama was running for Illinois' U.S. Senate seat, a relative newcomer to the national political scene. Still, he wasted no time reshaping his party's message in the keynote address to the 2004 Democratic National Convention. In the previous months, the Democratic candidates had campaigned on the idea that there were "two different Americas, one for all those who are in positions of power and privilege…and one for everybody else."

Speaking to the Tuesday night audience, Obama extolled the ideals that form a common bond among all Americans, emphasizing the *unity* of our nation over its divisions. He poked fun at the pundits who divide the electoral map into Red States and Blue States, saying there was only one *United* States of America.

By Thursday night, the new metaphor had found its way into the Democratic campaign script. As Senator John Kerry accepted the nomination, he paraphrased Obama's rhetoric: "Maybe some just see us divided into those Red States and Blue States, but I see us as one America: red, white, and blue." It became a mainstay for the rest of the campaign. John Kerry did not win that election, but Barack Obama won *his* race in Illinois and moved another step closer to the White House.

Answering a Call from Across the Generations

Obama's 2005 speech at the gala celebration of Congressman John Lewis' sixty-fifth birthday provided some early clues to the kind of presidential campaign he would soon be running. The occasion was a natural opportunity to reflect on the civil rights movement forty years earlier, and Obama used his own story as evidence that great change had come to America since the 1960s.

The lesson to be learned from Lewis' work, Obama said, was that change must come "from great discipline and organization, from a strong message of hope, and from the courage to turn against the tide so that the tide eventually may be turned." The words aptly describe his successful campaign for the White House.

"A Prayer Worth Praying, a Conversation Worth Having"

In 2004, Obama's opponent had made religion a divisive issue in the U.S. Senate campaign, even going so far as to say, "Jesus Christ would not vote for Barack Obama." Answering the attack in a conventional way, Obama described religion as a personal matter, one that had no bearing on his commitment to the state of Illinois. After the election, he decided to address the issue more directly by exploring the ways in which faith influenced his value system and drove him to want to help others and participate in a larger community.

As keynote speaker at a Call to Renewal conference in 2006, Obama suggested that Democrats should not be afraid to address the issue of religion head-on. Focusing on the common aspects of religion as a bond among us, instead of a force that divides us, he warned secularists that asking politicians to "leave their religion at the door" would "forfeit the imagery and terminology through which millions of Americans understand both their personal morality and social justice." At the same time, he cited the need for religious groups to translate their "concerns into universal, rather than religion-specific values."

Without compromising the bedrock principle of the separation of church and state, Obama managed to forge a novel approach to incorporating the power of his faith into the political conversation—one that would allow him to avoid ceding the Evangelical Christian vote to his opponents in future elections.

Calling Upon Our Better Angels

Speaking at the dedication of the Abraham Lincoln Presidential Library and Museum in Springfield, Illinois, in the spring of 2005, then-Senator Obama referred to the sixteenth president in iconic terms, calling him "the real thing," despite his weaknesses and flaws. "Lincoln embodies our deepest myths," Obama said. "It is a mythology that drives us still."

Nearly two years later, Obama returned to Springfield to announce that he would be running for president. There he began to lay out his vision for the future, starting with a call for "change," while reminding us that the "genius of our founders is that they designed a system of government that can be changed." Evoking the line in John F. Kennedy's inaugural address that said, "The torch has been passed to a new generation," Obama set forth four clear objectives for *his* generation to achieve: ending poverty, providing health care, achieving independence from foreign oil, and defeating terrorists to make America safe. Those goals, and his call to a new generation, became the corner-stones of his campaign platform.

The Road to Victory

As 2007 ended, Obama brought his message of change to Iowa, where the race for president would start in earnest and where victory in January 2008 made him a serious contender.

By the New Hampshire primary, the message of change had been distilled to three words that turned a defeat into a reason to press on: "Yes We Can."

In March, Obama addressed the issue of race by redefining it. Just as he had confronted questions of faith by advocating open dialogue, he called upon Americans to break out of the "racial stalemate we've been stuck in for years," to "move beyond some of the old racial wounds," and "to continue on the path of a more perfect union."

On August 28, 2008—exactly forty-five years after Dr. Martin Luther King spoke on the Mall in Washington, D.C., of his dream of equality—Barack Obama became the Democratic Party candidate for president. Accepting the nomination, Obama echoed Dr. King, calling on Americans to continue marching forward to fulfill a common dream: "America, we cannot turn back. We cannot walk alone."

"Change Has Come to America"

On Election Day, with financial collapse sweeping the globe, America and the world waited to learn the results of an unusually long and arduous race. That night, when President-elect Obama stepped onto the stage in Chicago, the transformation from candidate to Commander in Chief had unmistakably begun. His gait, his tone, and his words all reflected the profound nature of what had transpired that day.

Obama began with a simple message: "If there is anyone out there who still doubts that America is a place where all things are possible...tonight is your answer." From there, his speech combined the sounds of a politician (acknowledging his opponents as colleagues), a leader (thanking all those who had made his victory possible), and a human being (telling his daughters they would be bringing a new puppy with them to the White House).

Obama paid homage to the historical figures whose work had made the night possible. His victory was proof, he said, that Lincoln's government "of the people, by the people, and for the people" still flourished. Acknowledging that the road would be long and the climb steep, he nevertheless promised a brighter future with a refrain from Dr. King: "We as a people will get there." And, just as nearly half a century earlier President Kennedy had told Americans to "Ask what you can do for your country," Obama called for "a new spirit of patriotism; of service and responsibility."

And all that was simply the prelude to the moment when the art of American oratory made a triumphant return to the White House. In his inaugural address, President Obama combined an honest and sober account of the state of the nation with an optimistic vision of its destiny. Speaking of the ties that bind us, Obama identified "our patchwork heritage" as a source of strength. He called for all Americans to acknowledge that "we have duties to ourselves, our nation, and the world," referring to them as "the price and the promise of citizenship." In short, Barack Obama began his presidency in much the same way as he won it—using the power of his words to inspire the nation to listen, to reflect, and to move forward.

—VICTOR DORFF
January, 2009

BARACK OBAMA

WORDS THAT INSPIRED A NATION

Against Going to War with Iraq

Good afternoon. Let me begin by saying that although this has been billed as an antiwar rally, I stand before you as someone who is not opposed to war in all circumstances. The Civil War was one of the bloodiest in history, and yet it was only through the crucible of the sword, the sacrifice of multitudes, that we could begin to perfect this union, and drive the scourge of slavery from our soil. I don't oppose all wars.

My grandfather signed up for a war the day after Pearl Harbor was bombed, fought in Patton's army. He saw the dead and dying across the fields of Europe; he heard the stories of fellow troops who first entered Auschwitz and Treblinka. He fought in the name of a larger freedom, part of that arsenal of democracy that triumphed over evil, and he did not fight in vain. I don't oppose all wars.

After September 11th, after witnessing the carnage and destruction, the dust and the tears, I supported this administration's pledge to hunt down and root out those who would slaughter innocents in the name of intolerance, and I would willingly take up arms myself to prevent such tragedy from happening again. I don't oppose all wars. And I know that in this crowd today, there is no shortage of patriots, or of patriotism.

What I am opposed to is a dumb war. What I am opposed to is a rash war. What I am opposed to is the cynical attempt by Richard Perle and Paul Wolfowitz and other armchair, weekend warriors in this administration to shove their own ideological agendas down our throats, irrespective of the costs in lives lost and in hardships borne.

What I am opposed to is the attempt by political hacks like Karl Rove to distract us from a rise in the uninsured, a rise in the poverty rate, a drop in the median income—to distract us from corporate scandals and a stock market that has just gone through the worst month since the Great Depression. That's what I'm opposed to. A dumb war. A rash war. A war based not on reason but on passion, not on principle but on politics. Now let me be clear—I suffer no illusions about Saddam Hussein. He is a brutal man. A ruthless man. A man who butchers his own people to secure his own power. He has repeatedly defied UN resolutions, thwarted UN inspection teams, developed chemical and biological weapons, and coveted nuclear capacity. He's a bad guy. The world, and the Iraqi people, would be better off without him.

> " *Those are the battles that we need to fight. Those are the battles that we willingly join. The battles against ignorance and intolerance. Corruption and greed. Poverty and despair.* "

But I also know that Saddam poses no imminent and direct threat to the United States, or to his neighbors, that the Iraqi economy is in shambles, that the Iraqi military [is] a fraction of its former strength, and that in concert with the international community he can be contained until, in the way of all petty dictators, he falls away into the dustbin of history. I know that even a successful war against Iraq will require a U.S. occupation of undetermined length, at undetermined cost, with undetermined consequences. I know that an invasion of Iraq without a clear rationale and without strong international support will only fan the flames of the Middle East, and encourage the worst, rather than best, impulses of the Arab world, and strengthen the recruitment arm of Al Qaeda. I am not opposed to all wars. I'm opposed to dumb wars.

So for those of us who seek a more just and secure world for our children, let us send a clear message to the president today. You want a fight, President Bush? Let's finish the fight with Bin Laden and Al Qaeda, through effective, coordinated intelligence, and a shutting down of the financial networks that support terrorism, and a homeland security program that involves more than color-coded warnings. You want a fight, President Bush? Let's fight to make sure that the UN inspectors can do their work, and that we vigorously enforce a non-proliferation treaty, and that former enemies and current allies like Russia safeguard and ultimately eliminate their stores of nuclear material, and that nations like Pakistan and India never use the terrible weapons already in their possession, and that the arms merchants in our own country stop feeding the countless wars that rage across the globe. You want a fight, President Bush?

Let's fight to make sure our so-called allies in the Middle East, the Saudis and the Egyptians, stop oppressing their own people, and suppressing dissent, and tolerating corruption and inequality, and mismanaging their economies so that their youth grow up without education, without prospects, without hope, the ready recruits of terrorist cells. You want a fight, President Bush? Let's fight to wean ourselves off Middle East oil, through an energy policy that doesn't simply serve the interests of Exxon and Mobil. Those are the battles that we need to fight. Those are the battles that we willingly join. The battles against ignorance and intolerance. Corruption and greed. Poverty and despair.

The consequences of war are dire, the sacrifices immeasurable. We may have occasion in our lifetime to once again rise up in defense of our freedom, and pay the wages of war. But we ought not—we will not—travel down that hellish path blindly. Nor should we allow those who would march off and pay the ultimate sacrifice, who would prove the full measure of devotion with their blood, to make such an awful sacrifice in vain.

The Audacity of Hope

Keynote Address, 2004 Democratic National Convention

Boston, Massachusetts • July 27, 2004

On behalf of the great state of Illinois, crossroads of a nation, land of Lincoln, let me express my deep gratitude for the privilege of addressing this convention. Tonight is a particular honor for me because, let's face it, my presence on this stage is pretty unlikely. My father was a foreign student, born and raised in a small village in Kenya. He grew up herding goats, went to school in a tin-roof shack. His father, my grandfather, was a cook, a domestic servant.

But my grandfather had larger dreams for his son. Through hard work and perseverance my father got a scholarship to study in a magical place: America, which stood as a beacon of freedom and opportunity to so many who had come before. While studying here, my father met my mother. She was born in a town on the other side of the world, in Kansas. Her father worked on oil rigs and farms through most of the Depression. The day after Pearl Harbor he signed up for duty, joined Patton's army and marched across Europe. Back home, my grandmother raised their baby and went to work on a bomber assembly line. After the war, they studied on the GI Bill, bought a house through FHA, and moved west in search of opportunity.

And they, too, had big dreams for their daughter, a common dream, born of two continents. My parents shared not only an improbable love; they shared an abiding faith in the possibilities of this nation. They would give me an African name, Barack, or "blessed," believing that in a tolerant America your name is no barrier to success. They imagined me going to the best schools in the land, even though they weren't rich, because in a generous America you don't have to be rich to achieve your potential. They are both passed away now. Yet, I know that, on this night, they look down on me with pride.

I stand here today, grateful for the diversity of my heritage, aware that my parents' dreams live on in my precious daughters. I stand here knowing that my story is part of the larger American story, that I owe a debt to all of those who came before me, and that, in no other country on earth, is my story even possible. Tonight, we gather to affirm the greatness of our nation, not because of the height of our skyscrapers, or the power of our military, or the size of our economy. Our pride is based on a very simple premise, summed up in a declaration made over two hundred years ago, "We hold these truths to be self-evident, that all men are created equal. That they are endowed by their Creator with certain inalienable rights. That among these are life, liberty and the pursuit of happiness."

That is the true genius of America, a faith in the simple dreams of its people, the insistence on small miracles. That we can tuck in our children at night and know they are fed and clothed and safe from harm. That we can say what we think, write what we think, without hearing a sudden knock on the door. That we can have an idea and start our own business without paying a bribe or hiring somebody's son. That we can participate in the political process without fear of retribution, and that our votes will be counted—or at least, most of the time.

This year, in this election, we are called to reaffirm our values and commitments, to hold them against a hard reality and see how we are measuring up to the legacy of our forbearers and the promise of future generations. And fellow Americans—Democrats, Republicans, Independents—I say to you tonight: we have more work to do. More to do for the workers I met in Galesburg, Illinois, who are losing their union jobs at the Maytag plant that's moving to Mexico, and now are having to compete with their own children for jobs that pay seven bucks an hour. More to do for the father I met who was losing his job and choking back tears, wondering how he would pay $4,500 a month for the drugs his son needs without the health benefits he counted on. More to do for the young woman in East St. Louis, and thousands more like her, who has the grades, has the drive, has the will, but doesn't have the money to go to college.

Don't get me wrong. The people I meet in small towns and big cities, in diners and office parks, they don't expect government to solve all their problems. They know they have to work hard to get ahead and they want to. Go into the collar counties around Chicago, and people will tell you they don't want their tax money wasted by a welfare agency or the Pentagon. Go into any inner city neighborhood, and folks will tell you that government alone can't teach kids to learn. They know that parents have to parent, that children can't achieve unless we raise their expectations and turn off the television sets and eradicate the slander that says a black youth with a book is acting white. No, people don't expect government to solve all their problems. But they sense, deep in their bones, that with just a change in priorities, we can make sure that every child in America has a decent shot at life, and that the doors of opportunity remain open to all. They know we can do better. And they want that choice.

In this election, we offer that choice. Our party has chosen a man to lead us who embodies the best this country has to offer. That man is John Kerry. John

Kerry understands the ideals of community, faith, and sacrifice, because they've defined his life. From his heroic service in Vietnam to his years as prosecutor and lieutenant governor, through two decades in the United States Senate, he has devoted himself to this country. Again and again, we've seen him make tough choices when easier ones were available. His values and his record affirm what is best in us.

John Kerry believes in an America where hard work is rewarded. So instead of offering tax breaks to companies shipping jobs overseas, he'll offer them to companies creating jobs here at home.

> *"It's that fundamental belief—I am my brother's keeper, I am my sister's keeper—that makes this country work. It's what allows us to pursue our individual dreams, yet still come together as a single American family. 'E pluribus unum.' Out of many, one."*

John Kerry believes in an America where all Americans can afford the same health coverage our politicians in Washington have for themselves. John Kerry believes in energy independence, so we aren't held hostage to the profits of oil companies or the sabotage of foreign oil fields. John Kerry believes in the constitutional freedoms that have made our country the envy of the world, and he will never sacrifice our basic liberties nor use faith as a wedge to divide us. And John Kerry believes that in a dangerous world, war must be an option, but it should never be the first option.

A while back, I met a young man named Shamus at the VFW Hall in East Moline, Illinois. He was a good-looking kid, six-two or six-three, clear-eyed, with an easy smile. He told me he'd joined the Marines and was heading to Iraq the following week. As I listened to him explain why he'd enlisted, his absolute faith in our country and its leaders, his devotion to duty and service, I thought this young man was all any of us might hope for in a child. But then I asked myself: Are we serving Shamus as well as he was serving us? I thought of more than 900 service men and women, sons and daughters, husbands and wives, friends and neighbors, who will not be returning to their hometowns. I thought of families I had met who were struggling to get by without a loved one's full income, or whose loved ones had returned with a limb missing or with nerves shattered, but who still lacked long-term health benefits because they were reservists. When we send our young men and women into harm's way, we have a solemn obligation not to fudge the numbers or shade the truth about why they're going, to care for their families while they're gone, to tend to the soldiers upon their return, and to never ever go to war without enough troops to win the war, secure the peace, and earn the respect of the world.

> "Out of this long political darkness a brighter day will come."

Now let me be clear. We have real enemies in the world. These enemies must be found. They must be pursued and they must be defeated. John Kerry knows this. And just as Lieutenant Kerry did not hesitate to risk his life to protect the men who served with him in Vietnam, President Kerry will not hesitate one moment to use our military might to keep America safe and secure. John Kerry believes in America. And he knows it's not enough for just some of us to prosper. For alongside our famous individualism, there's another ingredient in the American saga. A belief that we are connected as one people. If there's a child on the south side of Chicago who can't read, that matters to me, even if it's not my child. If there's a senior citizen somewhere who can't pay for her prescription and has to choose between medicine and the rent, that makes my life poorer, even if it's not my grandmother. If there's an Arab-American family being rounded up without benefit of an attorney or due process, that threatens my civil liberties. It's that fundamental belief—I am my brother's keeper, I am my sister's keeper— that makes this country work. It's what allows us to pursue our individual dreams, yet still come together as a single American family. "E pluribus unum." Out of many, one.

Yet even as we speak, there are those who are preparing to divide us, the spin masters and negative ad peddlers who embrace the politics of anything goes. Well, I say to them tonight, there's not a liberal America and a conservative America—there's the United States of America. There's not a black America and white America and Latino America and Asian America; there's the United States of America. The pundits like to slice-and-dice our country into Red States and Blue States; Red States for Republicans, Blue States for Democrats. But I've got news for them, too. We worship an awesome God in the Blue States, and we don't like federal agents poking around our libraries in the Red States. We coach Little League in the Blue States and have gay friends in the Red States. There are patriots who opposed the war in Iraq and patriots who supported it. We are one people, all of us pledging allegiance to the stars and stripes, all of us defending the United States of America.

In the end, that's what this election is about. Do we participate in a politics of cynicism or a politics of hope? John Kerry calls on us to hope. John Edwards calls on us to hope. I'm not talking about blind optimism here—the almost willful ignorance that thinks unemployment will go away if we just don't talk about it, or the health care crisis will solve itself if we just ignore it. No, I'm talking about something more substantial. It's the hope of slaves sitting around a fire singing freedom songs; the hope of immigrants setting out for distant shores; the hope of a young naval lieutenant bravely patrolling the Mekong Delta; the hope of a millworker's son who dares to defy the odds; the hope of a skinny kid with a funny name who believes that America has a place for him, too. The audacity of hope! In the end, that is God's greatest gift to us, the bedrock of this nation: the belief in things not seen, the belief that there are better days ahead. I believe we can give our middle class relief and provide working families with a road to opportunity. I believe we can provide jobs to the jobless, homes to the homeless, and reclaim young people in cities across America from violence and despair.

I believe that as we stand on the crossroads of history, we can make the right choices, and meet the challenges that face us.

America! Tonight, if you feel the same energy I do, the same urgency I do, the same passion I do, the same hopefulness I do—if we do what we must do, then I have no doubt that all across the country, from Florida to Oregon, from Washington to Maine, the people will rise up in November, and John Kerry will be sworn in as president, and John Edwards will be sworn in as vice president, and this country will reclaim its promise, and out of this long political darkness a brighter day will come. Thank you and God bless you.

Birthday Tribute to John Lewis

ATLANTA, GEORGIA • FEBRUARY 21, 2005

Thank you. It's an honor to be here tonight to celebrate one of the most courageous and compassionate Americans of our time. Happy Birthday John.

When I was first asked to speak here, I thought to myself, never in a million years would I have guessed that I'd be serving in Congress with John Lewis.

And then I thought, you know, there was once a time when John Lewis might never have guessed that he'd be serving in Congress. And there was a time not long before that when people might never have guessed that someday, African-Americans would be able to go to the polls, pick up a ballot, make their voice heard, and elect that Congress.

But we can, and I'm here, because people like John Lewis believed. Because people like John Lewis feared nothing and risked everything for those beliefs.

> *"The road John chose for himself was not easy. But the road to change never is."*

Because they were willing to spend sleepless nights in lonely jail cells, endure the searing pain of billy clubs cracked against their bones, and face down death simply so that all of us could share equally in the joys of life.

How far we've come because of your courage, John.

How far we've come from the days when the son of sharecroppers would huddle by the radio as the crackle of Dr. King's dreams filled his heart with hope. He was often forced to leave school to work in the fields and the public library was off-limits to his kind, and yet young John Lewis sought knowledge. His parents were never the type to complain or try to stir up any trouble, and yet their son sought justice.

And so he organized, even when so many tried to stop his efforts. He spoke truths, even when they tried to silence his words. And he marched, even when they tried to knock him down again and again and again.

The road John chose for himself was not easy. But the road to change never is.

I think it's simple for us to look back forty years and think that it was all so clear then. That while there may be room for moral ambiguity in the issues we debate today, civil rights was different. That people generally knew what was right and what was wrong, who the good guys and the bad guys were. But the moral certainties we now take for granted—that separate can never be equal, that the blessings of liberty enshrined in our Constitution belong to all of us, that our children should be able to go to school together and play together and grow up together—were anything but certain when John Lewis was a boy.

And so there was struggle and sacrifice, discipline, and tremendous courage. And there was the culmination of it all one Sunday afternoon on a bridge in Alabama.

I've often thought about the people on the Edmund Pettus Bridge that day. Not only John and Hosea Williams leading the march, but the hundreds of everyday Americans who left their homes and their churches to join it. Blacks and whites, teenagers and children, teachers and bankers and shopkeepers—a beloved community of God's children ready to stand for freedom.

And I wonder, where did they find that kind of courage? When you're facing row after row of state troopers on horseback armed with billy clubs and tear gas…when they're coming toward you spewing hatred and violence, how do you simply stop, kneel down, and pray to the Lord for salvation? Truly, this is the audacity of hope.

But the most amazing thing of all is that after that day—after John Lewis was beaten within an inch of his life, after people's heads were gashed open and their eyes were burned and they watched their children's innocence literally beaten out of them…after all that, they went back to march again.

They marched again. They crossed the bridge. They awakened a nation's conscience, and not five months later, the Voting Rights Act of 1965 was signed into law.

And so it was, in a story as old as our beginnings and as timeless as our hopes, that change came about because the good people of a great nation willed it so.

Thank you, John, for going back. Thank you for marching again.

Thank you for reminding us that in America, ordinary citizens can somehow find in their hearts the courage to do extraordinary things. That in the face of the fiercest resistance and the most crushing oppression, one voice can be willing to stand up and say that's wrong and this is right and here's why. And say it again. And say it louder. And keep saying it until other voices join the chorus to sing the songs that set us free.

Today, I'm sure you'll all agree that we have songs left to sing and bridges left to cross. And if there's anything we can learn from this living saint sitting beside me, it is that change is never easy, but always possible. That it comes not from violence or militancy or the kind of politics that pits us against each other and plays on our worst fears; but from great discipline and organization, from a strong message of hope, and from the courage to turn against the tide so that the tide eventually may be turned.

Today, we need that courage. We need the courage to say that it's wrong that one out of every five children is born into poverty in the richest country on earth. And it's right to do whatever necessary to provide our children the care and the education they need to live up to their God-given potential.

It's wrong to tell hardworking families who are earning less and paying more in taxes that we can't do anything to help them buy their own home or send

---

their kids to college or care for them when they're sick. And it's right to expect that if you're willing to work hard in this country of American Dreamers, the sky is the limit on what you can achieve.

It's wrong to tell those brave men and women who are willing to fight and die for this country that when they come home, we may not have room for them at the VA hospitals or the benefits we promised them. And it's right to always provide the very best care for the very best of America.

My friends, we have not come this far as a people and a nation because we believe that we're better off simply fending for ourselves. We are here because we believe that all men are created equal, and that we are all connected to each other as one people. And we need to say that more. And say it again. And keep saying it.

> *"Martin Luther King, Jr. spoke to the crowd of thousands and said 'The arc of the moral universe is long, but it bends towards justice.' He's right, but you know what? It doesn't bend on its own. It bends because we help it bend that way."*

And where will our courage come from to speak these truths? When we stand on our own Edmund Pettus Bridge, what hope will sustain us?

I believe it is the hope of knowing that people like John Lewis have stood on that same bridge and lived to cross it.

For me, this kind of hope often comes from a memory of a trip I took during the campaign. About a week after the primary, Dick Durbin and I embarked on a nineteen-city tour of southern Illinois. And one of the towns we went to was a place called Cairo, which, as many of you might know, achieved a certain notoriety during the late '60s and early '70s as having one of the worst racial climates in the country. You had an active white citizen's council there, you had cross burnings, Jewish families were being harassed, you had segregated schools, race riots, you name it—it was going on in Cairo.

And we're riding down to Cairo and Dick Durbin turns to me and says, "Let me tell you about the first time I went to Cairo. It was about 30 years ago. I was 23 years old and Paul Simon, who was lieutenant governor at the time, sent me down there to investigate what could be done to improve the racial climate in Cairo."

And Dick tells me how he diligently goes down there and gets picked up by a local resident who takes him to his motel. And as Dick's getting out of the car, the driver says, "Excuse me, let me just give you a piece of advice. Don't use the phone in your motel room because the switchboard operator is a member of the white citizen's council, and they'll report on anything you do."

Well, this obviously makes Dick Durbin upset, but he's a brave young man, so he checks in to his room, unpacks his bags, and a few minutes later he hears a knock on the door. He opens up the door and there's a guy standing there who just stares at Dick for a second, and then says, "What the hell are you doing here?" and walks away.

Well, now Dick is really feeling concerned and so am I because as he's telling me this story, we're pulling in to Cairo. So I'm wondering what kind of reception we're going to get. And we wind our way through the town and we go past the old courthouse, take a turn, and suddenly we're in a big parking lot and about 300 people are standing there. About a fourth of them are black and three fourths are white and they all are about the age where they would have been active participants in the epic struggle that had taken place thirty years earlier.

And as we pull closer, I see something. All of these people are wearing these little buttons that say "Obama for U.S. Senate." And they start smiling. And they start waving. And Dick and I looked at each other and didn't have to say a thing. Because if you told Dick thirty years ago that he—the son of Lithuania immigrants born into very modest means in east St. Louis—would be returning to Cairo as a sitting United States Senator, and that he would have in tow a black guy born in Hawaii with a father from Kenya and a mother from Kansas named Barack Obama, no one would have believed it.

But it happened. And it happened because John Lewis and scores of brave Americans stood on that bridge and lived to cross it.

You know, two weeks after Bloody Sunday, when the march finally reached Montgomery, Martin Luther King, Jr. spoke to the crowd of thousands and said, "The arc of the moral universe is long, but it bends towards justice." He's right, but you know what? It doesn't bend on its own. It bends because we help it bend that way. Because people like John Lewis and Hosea Williams and Martin Luther King and Coretta Scott King and Rosa Parks and thousands of ordinary Americans with extraordinary courage have helped bend it that way. And as their examples call out to us from across the generations, we continue to progress as a people because they inspire us to take our own two hands and bend that arc. Thank you John. May God Bless you, and may God Bless these United States of America.

Our Better Angels

Opening of the Abraham Lincoln Presidential Library and Museum

SPRINGFIELD, ILLINOIS • APRIL 20, 2005

Let me congratulate all of those who have helped to make this wonderful vision a reality.

But we gather here today not to celebrate a building. We gather to celebrate a man.

What is it that makes Lincoln such a seminal figure in our story? How is it that this man, born in the backwoods of Kentucky, with little formal education, homely and awkward, a man given to depression and wracked with self-doubt, might come to represent so much of who we are as a people, and so much of what we aspire to be?

> *"It serves us then to reflect on whether that element of Lincoln's character, and the American character— that aspect which makes tough choices, and speaks the truth when least convenient, and acts while still admitting doubt— remains with us today."*

Some of it has to do with the trajectory of his life. In his rise from poverty, his self-study and ultimate mastery of language and of law, in his capacity to overcome personal loss and remain determined in the face of repeated defeat—in all of this we see a fundamental element of the American character, a belief that we can constantly remake ourselves to fit our larger dreams.

Some of it has to do with the sheer energy of the man, the railsplitter, ax-in-hand, looking out at a frontier of hope and possibility. Lincoln believed deeply in the American spirit of innovation and exploration that accepts no limits to the heights to which our nation might reach.

In all of this—the repeated acts of self-creation, the insistence that with sweated brow and calloused hands and focused will we can recast the wilderness of the American landscape and the American heart into something better, something finer—in all of this Lincoln embodies our deepest myths. It is a mythology that drives us still.

And yet what separates Lincoln from the other great men has to do with something else. It's an issue of character that speaks to us, of moral resolve. Lincoln was not a perfect man, nor a perfect president. By modern standards, his condemnation of slavery might be considered tentative, his Emancipation Proclamation more a military document than a clarion call for justice. He wasn't immune to political considerations; his temperament could be indecisive and morose.

And yet despite these imperfections, despite his fallibility…indeed, perhaps because of a painful self-awareness of his own failings, etched in every crease of his face and reflected in those haunted eyes…because of this essential humanity of his, when it came time to confront the greatest moral challenge this nation has ever faced, Lincoln did not flinch. He did not equivocate or duck or pass the challenge on to future generations. He did not demonize the fathers and sons who did battle on the other side, nor seek to diminish the terrible costs of his war. In the midst of slavery's dark storm and the complexities of governing a house divided, he kept his moral compass pointed firm and true.

It serves us then to reflect on whether that element of Lincoln's character, and the American character—that aspect which makes tough choices, and speaks the truth when least convenient, and acts while still admitting doubt—remains with us today. Lincoln once said that "character is like a tree and reputation like its shadow. The shadow is what we think of it; the tree is the real thing."

At a time when image all too often trumps substance, when our politics all too often feeds rather than bridges division, when the prospects of a poor youth rising out of poverty seem of no consequence to the powerful, and when we evoke our common God to condemn those who do not think as we do, rather than to seek God's mercy for our own lack of understanding—at such a time it is helpful to remember this man who was the real thing. Lincoln reminds us that our essential greatness is not the shadow of sophistication or popularity, or wealth or power or fleeting celebrity. It is the tree that stands in the face of our doubts and fears and bigotries, and insists we can do better.

Today we come to celebrate not a building but a man. And as that man called once upon the better angels of our nature, so is he calling still, across the ages, to summon some measure of that character, his character, in each of us, today.

The Power of Faith

Keynote Address, Call to Renewal Conference

WASHINGTON, D.C. • JUNE 28, 2006

Good morning. I appreciate the opportunity to speak here at the Call to Renewal's Building a Covenant for a New America conference. I've had the opportunity to take a look at your Covenant for a New America. It is filled with outstanding policies and prescriptions for much of what ails this country. So I'd like to congratulate you all on the thoughtful presentations you've given so far about poverty and justice in America, and for putting fire under the feet of the political leadership here in Washington.

But today I'd like to talk about the connection between religion and politics and perhaps offer some thoughts about how we can sort through some of the often bitter arguments that we've been seeing over the last several years.

I do so because, as you all know, we can affirm the importance of poverty in the Bible; and we can raise up and pass out this Covenant for a New America. We can talk to the press, and we can discuss the religious call to address poverty and environmental stewardship all we want, but it won't have an impact unless we tackle head-on the mutual suspicion that sometimes exists between religious America and secular America.

I want to give you an example that I think illustrates this fact. As some of you know, during the 2004 U.S. Senate General Election I ran against a gentleman named Alan Keyes. Mr. Keyes is well-versed in the Jerry Falwell-Pat Robertson style of rhetoric that often labels progressives as both immoral and godless.

Indeed, Mr. Keyes announced towards the end of the campaign that, "Jesus Christ would not vote for Barack Obama. Christ would not vote for Barack Obama because Barack Obama has behaved in a way that it is inconceivable for Christ to have behaved."

Jesus Christ would not vote for Barack Obama.

Now, I was urged by some of my liberal supporters not to take this statement seriously, to essentially ignore it. To them, Mr. Keyes was an extremist, and his arguments not worth entertaining. And since at the time, I was up 40 points in the polls, it probably wasn't a bad piece of strategic advice.

But what they didn't understand, however, was that I had to take Mr. Keyes seriously, for he claimed to speak for my religion, and my God. He claimed knowledge of certain truths.

Mr. Obama says he's a Christian, he was saying, and yet he supports a lifestyle that the Bible calls an abomination.

Mr. Obama says he's a Christian, but supports the destruction of innocent and sacred life.

And so what would my supporters have me say? How should I respond? Should I say that a literalist reading of the Bible was folly? Should I say that Mr. Keyes, who is a Roman Catholic, should ignore the teachings of the Pope?

Unwilling to go there, I answered with what has come to be the typically liberal response in such debates—namely, I said that we live in a pluralistic society, that I can't impose my own religious views on another, that I was running to be the U.S. Senator of Illinois and not the Minister of Illinois.

But Mr. Keyes's implicit accusation that I was not a true Christian nagged at me, and I was also aware that my answer did not adequately address the role my faith has in guiding my own values and my own beliefs.

Now, my dilemma was by no means unique. In a way, it reflected the broader debate we've been having in this country for the last thirty years over the role of religion in politics.

For some time now, there has been plenty of talk among pundits and pollsters that the political divide in this country has fallen sharply along religious lines. Indeed, the single biggest "gap" in party affiliation among white Americans today is not between men and women, or those who reside in so-called Red States and those who reside in Blue, but between those who attend church regularly and those who don't.

Conservative leaders have been all too happy to exploit this gap, consistently reminding evangelical Christians that Democrats disrespect their values and dislike their Church, while suggesting to the rest of the country that religious

Americans care only about issues like abortion and gay marriage; school prayer and intelligent design.

Democrats, for the most part, have taken the bait. At best, we may try to avoid the conversation about religious values altogether, fearful of offending anyone and claiming that—regardless of our personal beliefs—constitutional principles tie our hands. At worst, there are some liberals who dismiss religion in the public square as inherently irrational or intolerant, insisting on a caricature of religious Americans that paints them as fanatical, or thinking that the very word "Christian" describes one's political opponents, not people of faith.

Now, such strategies of avoidance may work for progressives when our opponent is Alan Keyes. But over the long haul, I think we make a mistake when we fail to acknowledge the power of faith in people's lives—in the lives of the American people—and I think it's time that we join a serious debate about how to reconcile faith with our modern, pluralistic democracy.

> *"Faith doesn't mean that you don't have doubts."*

And if we're going to do that then we first need to understand that Americans are a religious people. Ninety percent of us believe in God, 70 percent affiliate themselves with an organized religion, 38 percent call themselves committed Christians, and substantially more people in America believe in angels than [they do] in evolution.

This religious tendency is not simply the result of successful marketing by skilled preachers or the draw of popular mega-churches. In fact, it speaks to a hunger that's deeper than that—a hunger that goes beyond any particular issue or cause.

Each day, it seems, thousands of Americans are going about their daily rounds—dropping off the kids at school, driving to the office, flying to a business meeting, shopping at the mall, trying to stay on their diets—and they're coming to the realization that something is missing. They are deciding that their work, their possessions, their diversions, their sheer busyness, is not enough.

They want a sense of purpose, a narrative arc to their lives. They're looking to relieve a chronic loneliness, a feeling supported by a recent study that shows Americans have fewer close friends and confidants than ever before. And so they need an assurance that somebody out there cares about them, is listening to them—that they are not just destined to travel down that long highway towards nothingness.

And I speak with some experience on this matter. I was not raised in a particularly religious household, as undoubtedly many in the audience were. My father, who returned to Kenya when I was just two, was born Muslim but as an adult became an atheist. My mother, whose parents were non-practicing Baptists and Methodists, was probably one of the most spiritual and kindest people I've ever known, but grew up with a healthy skepticism of organized religion herself. As a consequence, so did I.

It wasn't until after college, when I went to Chicago to work as a community organizer for a group of Christian churches, that I confronted my own spiritual dilemma.

I was working with churches, and the Christians who I worked with recognized themselves in me. They saw that I knew their Book and that I shared their values and sang their songs. But they sensed that a part of me remained removed, detached, that I was an observer in their midst.

And in time, I came to realize that something was missing as well—that without a vessel for my beliefs, without a commitment to a particular community of faith, at some level I would always remain apart, and alone.

And if it weren't for the particular attributes of the historically black church, I may have accepted this fate. But as the months passed in Chicago, I found myself drawn—not just to work with the church, but to be in the church.

For one thing, I believed and still believe in the power of the African-American religious tradition to spur social change, a power made real by some of the leaders here today. Because of its past, the black church understands in an intimate way the Biblical call to feed the hungry and cloth the naked and challenge powers and principalities. And in its historical struggles for freedom and the rights of man, I was able to see faith as more than just a comfort to the weary or a hedge against death, but rather as an active, palpable agent in the world. As a source of hope.

And perhaps it was out of this intimate knowledge of hardship—the grounding of faith in struggle—that the church offered me a second insight, one that I think is important to emphasize today.

Faith doesn't mean that you don't have doubts.

You need to come to church in the first place precisely because you are first of this world, not apart from it. You need to embrace Christ precisely because you have sins to wash away—because you are human and need an ally in this difficult journey.

It was because of these newfound understandings that I was finally able to walk down the aisle of Trinity United Church of Christ on 95th Street in the Southside of Chicago one day and affirm my Christian faith. It came about as a choice, and not an epiphany. I didn't fall out in church. The questions I had didn't magically disappear. But kneeling beneath that cross on the South Side, I felt that I heard God's spirit beckoning me. I submitted myself to His will, and dedicated myself to discovering His truth.

That's a path that has been shared by millions upon millions of Americans—evangelicals, Catholics, Protestants, Jews, and Muslims alike; some since birth, others at certain turning points in their lives. It is not something they set apart from the rest of their beliefs and values. In fact, it is often what drives their beliefs and their values.

And that is why that, if we truly hope to speak to people where they're at—to communicate our hopes and values in a way that's relevant to their own—then as progressives, we cannot abandon the field of religious discourse.

Because when we ignore the debate about what it means to be a good Christian or Muslim or Jew; when we discuss religion only in the negative sense of where or how it should not be practiced, rather than in the positive sense of what it tells us about our obligations towards one another; when we shy away from religious venues and religious broadcasts because we assume that we will be unwelcome—others will fill the vacuum, those with the most insular views of faith, or those who cynically use religion to justify partisan ends.

In other words, if we don't reach out to evangelical Christians and other religious Americans and tell them what we stand for, then the Jerry Falwells and Pat Robertsons and Alan Keyeses will continue to hold sway.

More fundamentally, the discomfort of some progressives with any hint of religion has often prevented us from effectively addressing issues in moral terms. Some of the problem here is rhetorical—if we scrub language of all religious content, we forfeit the imagery and terminology through which millions of Americans understand both their personal morality and social justice.

Imagine Lincoln's Second Inaugural Address without reference to "the judgments of the Lord." Or King's *I Have a Dream* speech without references to "all of God's children." Their summoning of a higher truth helped inspire what had seemed impossible, and move the nation to embrace a common destiny.

Our failure as progressives to tap into the moral underpinnings of the nation is not just rhetorical, though. Our fear of getting "preachy" may also lead us to discount the role that values and culture play in some of our most urgent social problems.

> **"We might recognize that the call to sacrifice on behalf of the next generation, the need to think in terms of 'thou' and not just 'I,' resonates in religious congregations all across the country."**

After all, the problems of poverty and racism, the uninsured and the unemployed, are not simply technical problems in search of the perfect ten-point plan. They are rooted in both societal indifference and individual callousness—in the imperfections of man.

Solving these problems will require changes in government policy, but it will also require changes in hearts and a change in minds. I believe in keeping guns out of our inner cities, and that our leaders must say so in the face of the gun manufacturers' lobby—but I also believe that when a gang-banger shoots indiscriminately into a crowd because he feels somebody disrespected him, we've got a moral problem. There's a hole in that young man's heart—a hole that the government alone cannot fix.

I believe in vigorous enforcement of our non-discrimination laws. But I also believe that a transformation of conscience and a genuine commitment to diversity on the part of the nation's CEOs could bring about quicker results than a battalion of lawyers. They have more lawyers than us anyway.

I think that we should put more of our tax dollars into educating poor girls and boys. I think that the work that Marian Wright Edelman has done all her life is absolutely how we should prioritize our resources in the wealthiest nation on earth. I also think that we should give them the information about contraception that can prevent unwanted pregnancies, lower abortion rates, and help assure that that every child is loved and cherished.

But, you know, my Bible tells me that if we train a child in the way he should go, when he is old he will not turn from it. So I think faith and guidance can help fortify a young woman's sense of self, a young man's sense of responsibility, and a sense of reverence that all young people should have for the act of sexual intimacy.

I am not suggesting that every progressive suddenly latch on to religious terminology—that can be dangerous. Nothing is more transparent than inauthentic expressions of faith. As Jim [Wallis] has mentioned, some politicians come and clap—off rhythm—to the choir. We don't need that.

In fact, because I do not believe that religious people have a monopoly on morality, I would rather have someone who is grounded in morality and ethics, and who is also secular, affirm their morality and ethics and values without pretending that they're something they're not. They don't need to do that. None of us need to do that.

But what I am suggesting is this—secularists are wrong when they ask believers to leave their religion at the door before entering into the public square. Frederick Douglas, Abraham Lincoln, Williams Jennings Bryant, Dorothy Day,

Martin Luther King—indeed, the majority of great reformers in American history—were not only motivated by faith, but repeatedly used religious language to argue for their cause. So to say that men and women should not inject their "personal morality" into public policy debates is a practical absurdity. Our law is by definition a codification of morality, much of it grounded in the Judeo-Christian tradition.

Moreover, if we progressives shed some of these biases, we might recognize some overlapping values that both religious and secular people share when it comes to the moral and material direction of our country. We might recognize that the call to sacrifice on behalf of the next generation, the need to think in terms of "thou" and not just "I," resonates in religious congregations all across the country. And we might realize that we have the ability to reach out to the evangelical community and engage millions of religious Americans in the larger project of American renewal.

Some of this is already beginning to happen. Pastors, friends of mine like Rick Warren and T.D. Jakes, are wielding their enormous influences to confront AIDS, Third World debt relief, and the genocide in Darfur. Religious thinkers and activists like our good friend Jim Wallis and Tony Campolo are lifting up the Biblical injunction to help the poor as a means of mobilizing Christians against budget cuts to social programs and growing inequality.

And by the way, we need Christians on Capitol Hill, Jews on Capitol Hill, and Muslims on Capitol Hill talking about the estate tax. When you've got an estate tax debate that proposes a trillion dollars being taken out of social programs to go to a handful of folks who don't need and weren't even asking for it, you know that we need an injection of morality in our political debate.

Across the country, individual churches like my own and your own are sponsoring day care programs, building senior centers, helping ex-offenders reclaim their lives, and rebuilding our Gulf Coast in the aftermath of Hurricane Katrina.

So the question is, how do we build on these still-tentative partnerships between religious and secular people of good will? It's going to take more work, a lot more work than we've done so far. The tensions and the suspicions on each side of the religious divide will have to be squarely addressed. And each side will need to accept some ground rules for collaboration.

While I've already laid out some of the work that progressive leaders need to do, I want to talk a little bit about what conservative leaders need to do—some truths they need to acknowledge.

For one, they need to understand the critical role that the separation of church and state has played in preserving not only our democracy, but the robustness of our religious practice. Folks tend to forget that during our founding, it wasn't the atheists or the civil libertarians who were the most effective champions of the First Amendment. It was the persecuted minorities, it was Baptists like John Leland who didn't want the established churches to impose their views on folks who were getting happy out in the fields and teaching the scripture to slaves. It was the forbearers of the evangelicals who were the most adamant about not mingling government with religious, because they did not want state-sponsored religion hindering their ability to practice their faith as they understood it.

> "Politics depends on our ability to persuade each other of common aims based on a common reality. It involves the compromise, the art of what's possible."

Moreover, given the increasing diversity of America's population, the dangers of sectarianism have never been greater. Whatever we once were, we are no longer just a Christian nation; we are also a Jewish nation, a Muslim nation, a Buddhist nation, a Hindu nation, and a nation of nonbelievers.

And even if we did have only Christians in our midst, if we expelled every non-Christian from the United States of America, whose Christianity would we teach in the schools? Would we go with James Dobson's, or Al Sharpton's? Which passages of Scripture should guide our public policy? Should we go with Leviticus, which suggests slavery is ok and that eating shellfish is abomination? How about Deuteronomy, which suggests stoning your child if he strays from the faith? Or should we just stick to the Sermon on the Mount—a passage that is so radical that it's doubtful that our own Defense Department would survive its application? So before we get carried away, let's read our bibles. Folks haven't been reading their bibles.

This brings me to my second point. Democracy demands that the religiously motivated translate their concerns into universal, rather than religion-specific, values. It requires that their proposals be subject to argument, and amenable to reason. I may be opposed to abortion for religious reasons, but if I seek to pass a law banning the practice, I cannot simply point to the teachings of my church or evoke God's will. I have to explain why abortion violates some principle that is accessible to people of all faiths, including those with no faith at all.

Now this is going to be difficult for some who believe in the inerrancy of the Bible, as many evangelicals do. But in a pluralistic democracy, we have no choice. Politics depends on our ability to persuade each other of common aims based on a common reality. It involves the compromise, the art of what's possible. At some fundamental level, religion does not allow for compromise. It's the art of the impossible. If God has spoken, then followers are expected to live up to God's edicts, regardless of the consequences. To base one's life on such uncompromising commitments may be sublime, but to base our policy making on such commitments would be a dangerous thing. And if you doubt that, let me give you an example.

We all know the story of Abraham and Isaac. Abraham is ordered by God to offer up his only son, and without argument, he takes Isaac to the mountaintop, binds him to an altar, and raises his knife, prepared to act as God has commanded.

Of course, in the end God sends down an angel to intercede at the very last minute, and Abraham passes God's test of devotion.

But it's fair to say that if any of us leaving this church saw Abraham on a roof of a building raising his knife, we would, at the very least, call the police and expect the Department of Children and Family Services to take Isaac away from Abraham. We would do so because we do not hear what Abraham hears, do not see what Abraham sees, true as those experiences may be. So the best we can do is act in accordance with those things that we all see, and that we all hear, be it common laws or basic reason.

Finally, any reconciliation between faith and democratic pluralism requires some sense of proportion.

This goes for both sides.

Even those who claim the Bible's inerrancy make distinctions between Scriptural edicts, sensing that some passages—the Ten Commandments, say, or a belief in Christ's divinity—are central to Christian faith, while others are more culturally specific and may be modified to accommodate modern life.

The American people intuitively understand this, which is why the majority of Catholics practice birth control and some of those opposed to gay marriage nevertheless are opposed to a Constitutional amendment to ban it. Religious leadership need not accept such wisdom in counseling their flocks, but they should recognize this wisdom in their politics.

But a sense of proportion should also guide those who police the boundaries between church and state. Not every mention of God in public is a breach to the wall of separation—context matters. It is doubtful that children reciting the Pledge of Allegiance feel oppressed or brainwashed as a consequence of muttering the phrase "under God." I didn't. Having voluntary student prayer groups use school property to meet should not be a threat, any more than its use by the High School Republicans should threaten Democrats. And one can envision certain faith-based programs—targeting ex-offenders or substance abusers—that offer a uniquely powerful way of solving problems.

So we all have some work to do here. But I am hopeful that we can bridge the gaps that exist and overcome the prejudices each of us bring to this debate. And I have faith that millions of believing Americans want that to happen. No matter how religious they may or may not be, people are tired of seeing faith used as a tool of attack. They don't want faith used to belittle or to divide. They're tired of hearing folks deliver more screed than sermon. Because in the end, that's not how they think about faith in their own lives.

So let me end with just one other interaction I had during my campaign. A few days after I won the Democratic nomination in my U.S. Senate race, I received an e-mail from a doctor at the University of Chicago Medical School that said the following:

> Congratulations on your overwhelming and inspiring primary win. I was happy to vote for you, and I will tell you that I am seriously considering voting for you in the general election. I write to express my concerns that may, in the end, prevent me from supporting you.

The doctor described himself as a Christian who understood his commitments to be "totalizing." His faith led him to a strong opposition to abortion and gay marriage, although he said that his faith also led him to question the idolatry of the free market and quick resort to militarism that seemed to characterize much of the Republican agenda.

But the reason the doctor was considering not voting for me was not simply my position on abortion. Rather, he had read an entry that my campaign had posted on my website, which suggested that I would fight "right-wing ideologues who want to take away a woman's right to choose." The doctor went on to write:

> I sense that you have a strong sense of justice…and I also sense that you are a fair-minded person with a high regard for reason… Whatever your convictions, if you truly believe that those who oppose abortion are all ideologues driven by perverse desires to inflict suffering on women, then you, in my judgment, are not fair-minded… You know that we enter times that are fraught with possibilities for good and for harm, times when we are struggling to make sense of a common polity in the context of plurality, when we are unsure of what grounds we have for making any claims that involve others… I do not ask at this point that you oppose abortion, only that you speak about this issue in fair-minded words.

Fair-minded words.

So I looked at my website and found the offending words. In fairness to them, my staff had written them using standard Democratic boilerplate language to summarize my pro-choice position during the Democratic primary, at a time when some of my opponents were questioning my commitment to protect Roe v. Wade.

Re-reading the doctor's letter, though, I felt a pang of shame. It is people like him who are looking for a deeper, fuller conversation about religion in this country. They may not change their positions, but they are willing to listen and learn from those who are willing to speak in fair-minded words. Those who know of the central and awesome place that God holds in the lives of so many, and who refuse to treat faith as simply another political issue with which to score points.

So I wrote back to the doctor, and I thanked him for his advice. The next day, I circulated the e-mail to my staff and changed the language on my website to state in clear but simple terms my pro-choice position. And that night, before I went to bed, I said a prayer of my own—a prayer that I might extend the same presumption of good faith to others that the doctor had extended to me.

And that night, before I went to bed I said a prayer of my own. It's a prayer I think I share with a lot of Americans. A hope that we can live with one another in a way that reconciles the beliefs of each with the good of all. It's a prayer worth praying, and a conversation worth having in this country in the months and years to come. Thank you.

A Nation of No More Katrinas

Xavier University Commencement Address

New Orleans, Louisiana • August 11, 2006

Good afternoon President Francis, the Board of Trustees, faculty, parents, family, friends, and the Class of 2006.

I want to start by thanking you all for allowing me to share in your miracle today. Over the past year there has been no shortage of doubts about whether this college would live to see another commencement—and doubts remain still about the future of this great city. But on this summer's day in New Orleans, less than one year after the worst storm in American history beat down your door, I look out at the largest class to ever graduate from this college and know that one thing is certain—Xavier University is back.

I have to say that I'm pretty humbled to be here. Each year there are hundreds of commencements in this country. All are hopeful, some are inspiring, and most of you probably won't even remember who your speaker was ten years from now. As a rule, they usually involve an old guy like me giving young folks like you advice about what to expect in the real world—advice about the challenges you'll face and the obstacles you'll have to overcome.

But this is different. In the last month, I have walked among New Orleans' battered homes and empty

> *"It dawned on me that when it comes to giving advice about challenges and obstacles, it's you who could probably teach the rest of us a thing or two about what it takes to overcome."*

streets and scattered debris that prove armies aren't the only ones who can wage wars on cities. I have seen pictures of Xavier after the storm—the submerged classrooms and the shattered windows and the dorm rooms that were left with books sitting open on desks and clothes still unpacked on the bed. And I have heard the story of nearly 400 students and faculty who were trapped on campus in the days after Katrina—waiting on the roof to be rescued with a sign that simply read "Help Us."

And as I thought about all of this, it dawned on me that when it comes to giving advice about challenges and obstacles, it's you who could probably teach the rest of us a thing or two about what it takes to overcome.

I could give you a lecture on courage, but some of you know what it is to wait huddled in the dark without electricity or running water, wondering if a helicopter or boat will come for you before the gunshots get closer or the food runs out or the waters rise.

I could talk at length about perseverance, but this is a class that was forced to scatter to schools across the country at the beginning of your senior year, leaving everything you knew behind while you waited to find out if you could ever come back.

> "Remember always that while many in Washington and on all levels of government failed New Orleans, there were plenty of ordinary people who displayed extraordinary humanity during this city's hour of need."

And I could go on and on about the importance of community—about what it means to care for each other—but this is a school where so many sacrificed so much in order to open your doors in January; a triumph that showed the rest of America that there are those who refuse to desert this city and its people no matter what.

Yours has been an education that cannot simply be measured in the tests you've taken or the diploma you're about to receive. For it has also been an education in humanity, brought about by a force of nature—a lesson in both our capacity for good and in the imperfections of man; in our ability to rise to great challenges and our tendency to sometimes fall short of our obligations to one another.

Some will take an entire lifetime to experience these lessons—others never will. But as some of Katrina's youngest survivors, you've had a front row seat.

So what does this mean for you?

Well, lessons can be just as easily unlearned as they are learned. Time may heal, but it can also cloud the memory and remove us further from that initial core of concern.

And so what this all means is that today and every day, you have a responsibility to remember what happened here in New Orleans. To make it a part of who you are. To let its lessons guide you as you face your own challenges.

After all, Katrina may well be the most dramatic test you face in life, but it will by no means be the last. There will be quiet tests of character—the shoulder you lend a friend during their time of need; the way you raise your children; the care you give a loved one who's sick or dying; the integrity and honesty with which you carry yourself.

There will be powerful personal tests—the profession you choose, the legacy you leave, your ability to handle failure and disappointment.

And of course, there are the tests you will face as citizen—whether you use your voice to rage against injustice; whether you use your time to give back to your community; whether you use your passion to commit yourself to a cause larger than yourself.

In most of these tests, there are two different paths you can take.

One is easy. After graduating from a great school like Xavier, you'll pretty much be able to punch your own ticket—which means you can take your diploma, walk off this stage, leave this city, and go chasing after the big house and the large salary, and the nice suits, and all the other things that our money culture says you should buy.

You can live in neighborhoods with people who are exactly like yourself, and send your kids to the same schools, and narrow your concerns to what's going in your own little circle.

And when you turn on the TV or open the newspaper and hear about all the trouble in the world, there will be pundits and politicians who'll tell you that it's someone else's fault and someone else's problem to fix.

They'll tell you that the Americans who sleep in the streets and beg for food got there because they're all lazy or weak of spirit. That the immigrants who risk their lives to cross a desert have nothing to contribute to this country and no desire to embrace our ideals. That the inner-city children who are trapped in dilapidated schools can't learn and won't learn and so we should just give up on them entirely. That the innocent people being slaughtered and expelled from their homes in Darfur are somebody else's problem to take care of.

And when you hear all this, the easiest thing in the world will be to do nothing at all. To turn off the TV, put down the paper, and walk away from the stories about Iraq or poverty or violence or joblessness or hopelessness. To go about your busy lives—to remain detached; to remain indifferent; to remain safe.

But if you should ever think about taking this path, I ask you first to remember.

Remember witnessing the pain that neglect and indifference can cause—how entire neighborhoods in this city were left to drown because no one thought to make sure that every person had the means to escape. Remember what happens when responsibilities are ignored and bucks are passed—when the White House blames FEMA and FEMA blames the state of Louisiana and pretty soon no one's fixing the problem because everyone thought somebody else would. And whenever you're tempted to view the poor or the ill or the per-secuted as "those people"—people in their own world with their own prob-lems—remember always your neighbors in places like the 9th ward; men and women and children who, just like you, wanted desperately to escape to some-where better.

And if you remember all of this—if you remember what happened here in New Orleans—if you allow it to change you forever—know that there is another path you can take.

This one is more difficult. It asks more of you. It asks you to leave here and not just pursue your own individual dreams, but to help perfect our collective dream as a nation. It asks you to realize there is more to life than being rich, thin, young, famous, safe, and entertained. It asks you to recognize that there are people out there who need you.

You know, there's a lot of talk in this country about the federal deficit. But I think we should talk more about our empathy deficit—the ability to put ourselves in someone else's shoes; to see the world through the eyes of those who are different from us—the child who's hungry, the steelworker who's been laid-off, the family who lost the entire life they built together when the storm came to town.

> *"I ask you to take this harder path because you have an obligation to yourself. Because our individual salvation depends on our collective salvation."*

When you think like this—when you choose to broaden your ambit of concern and empathize with the plight of others, whether they are close friends or distant strangers—it becomes harder not to act; harder not to help.

For each of you, this desire to do for others and serve your communities will come even easier if you allow yourself to remember what you saw here in New Orleans.

Because aside from all the bad that came from Katrina—the failures and the neglect, the incompetence and the apathy—you were also witness to a good that many forgot was even possible.

You saw people from every corner of this country drop what they were doing, leave their homes, and come to New Orleans—Americans who didn't know a soul in the entire city who found their own piece of driftwood, built their own make-shift raft, and waded through the streets of this city, saving anyone they could.

You saw the doctors and the nurses who refused to leave their city and their patients even when they were told time and again by local officials that it was no longer safe—even when helicopters were waiting to take them away. Men and women who stayed to care for the sick and dying long after their medical equipment and electricity were gone.

And after the storm had passed, you saw a spirit of generosity that spanned an entire globe, with billions upon billions in donations coming from tiny, far-off nations like Qatar and Sri Lanka. Think about that. These are places a lot of folks couldn't even identify on a map. Sri Lanka was still recovering from the devastation caused by last year's tsunami. And yet, they heard about our tragedy, and they gave.

Remember always this goodness. Remember always that while many in Washington and on all levels of government failed New Orleans, there were plenty of ordinary people who displayed extraordinary humanity during this city's hour of need.

In the years to come, return this favor to those who are forced to weather their own storms—be it the loss of a job or a slide into poverty; an unexpected illness or an unforeseen eviction. And in returning these favors, seek also to make this a nation of no more Katrinas. Make this a nation where we never again leave behind any American by ensuring that every American has a job that can support a family and health care in case they get sick and a good education for their child and a secure retirement they can count on. Make this a nation where we are never again caught unprepared to meet the challenges of our time—where we free ourselves from a dependence on oil and protect our cities from both forces of terror and nature.

Make this a nation that is worthy of the sacrifices of so many of its citizens, and in doing so, make real the observation made by a visitor to our country so many centuries ago: "America is great because Americans are good."

I ask you to take this second path—this harder path—not because you have an obligation to those who are less fortunate, although you do have that obligation. Not because you have a debt to all of those who helped you get to where you are, although you do have that debt.

I ask you to take it because you have an obligation to yourself. Because our individual salvation depends on our collective salvation. And because it's only when you hitch your wagon to something larger than yourself that you will realize your true potential.

It is said that faith is a belief in things not seen, and miracles, by their nature, are inexplicable gifts from God.

But sometimes, if we look hard enough at the moments we triumph against the greatest of odds, we can see His will at work in the people He loves.

It's now well-known in this community that when your president, Norman Francis, promised to re-open this school by January, he joked that his decision would be recorded by history as either "crazy and stupid" or "bold and visionary."

And when I heard that, I wondered where you find the courage to make such a crazy, visionary promise—and where you find the commitment to keep it.

And I thought, Norman Francis is someone who remembers—remembers where he came from, remembers the lessons he learned, remembers the opportunities he's had, and lives his life according to those memories.

Born in Lafayette before Civil Rights and Voting Rights were even a possibility, this is a man who was raised in poverty, earning extra money for his parents as a child by shining shoes. He studied hard through high school, put himself through Xavier by working long hours in the library, and became the first ever African American to be accepted into Loyola's Law School.

He graduated that law school and could've gone anywhere and made any amount of money—but Norman Francis wanted to help people learn because he remembered all the people who helped him.

And so he came back to Xavier, and he worked his way up through the ranks, and he became the first ever African-American president of this school at just thirty-six years old.

Since that day he has had many accolades and many chances to do whatever he wished with his life. He has been an advisor to four U.S. Presidents, served on a commission to the Vatican, and as president of the United Negro College Fund.

But through all of this, he decided to stay here in New Orleans, and build this university.

And so when Katrina tried to tear it down, you can understand why he refused to let that happen—why he put aside tending to the damage in his own house so that he could work on rebuilding this one—why he believed more than anything in his promise that these doors would open in January.

Norman Francis has helped make today's miracle because he has seen miracles at work in his own life. Now that you have seen one in yours, it's your turn to live a life committed to others, devoted to the impossible, and ever aware of the lessons you learned in New Orleans.

I've noticed that in the rebuilding effort throughout this city, one of the last things to come back, and yet the easiest to notice, is the greenery that makes any community seem alive. And as I saw a newly planted tree on my last trip here, I thought of a passage from the book of Job:

> There is hope for a tree if it be cut down that it will sprout again, and that its tender branch will not cease.

Katrina was not the end of the tough times for New Orleans, and you will continue to face your own tests and challenges in the years to come. But if someone were to ask me how the tree stands on this August day, I would tell them that the seeds have sprouted, the roots are strong, and I just saw more than 500 branches that are ready to grow again. Congratulations on your graduation. Thank you.

An Honest Government, A Hopeful Future

NAIROBI, KENYA • AUGUST 28, 2006

The first time I came to Kenya was in 1987. I had just finished three years of work as a community organizer in low-income neighborhoods of Chicago, and was about to enroll in law school. My sister, Auma, was teaching that year at this university, and so I came to stay with her for a month.

My experience then was very different than it has been on this trip. Instead of a motorcade, we traveled in my sister's old VW Beetle, which even then was already ten years old. When it broke down in front of Uhuru Park, we had to push until some joakalis came to fix it by the side of the road. I slept on the couch of my sister's apartment, not a fancy hotel, and often took my meals at a small tea-house in downtown Nairobi. When we went upcountry, we traveled by train and matatu, with chickens and collard greens and sometimes babies placed in my lap.

> *"For all the progress that has been made, we must surely acknowledge that neither Kenya nor the African continent have yet fulfilled their potential."*

But it was a magical trip. To begin with, I discovered the warmth and sense of community that the people of Kenya possess—their sense of hopefulness even in the face of great difficulty. I discovered the beauty of the land, a beauty that haunts you long after you've left.

And most importantly for me, I discovered the story of my father's life, and the story of his father before him.

I learned that my grandfather had been a cook for the British and, although he was a respected elder in his village, he was called "boy" by his employers for most of his life. I learned about the brutal repression of Operation Anvil, the days of rape and torture in the "Pipeline" camps, the lives that so many gave, and how my grandfather had been arrested briefly during this period, despite being at the periphery of Kenya's liberation struggles.

I learned how my father had grown up in a tiny village called Alego, near Siaya, during this period of tumult. I began to understand and appreciate the distance he had traveled—from being a boy herding goats to a student at the University of Hawaii and Harvard University to the respected economist that he was upon his return to Kenya. In many ways, he embodied the new Africa of the early Sixties, a man who had obtained the knowledge of the Western world, and sought to bring it back home, where he hoped he could help create a new nation.

And yet, I discovered that for all his education, my father's life ended up being filled with disappointments. His ideas about how Kenya should progress often put him at odds with the politics of tribe and patronage, and because he spoke his mind, sometimes to a fault, he ended up being fired from his job and prevented from finding work in the country for many, many years. And on a more personal level, because he never fully reconciled the traditions of his village with more modern conceptions of family—because he related to women as his father had, expecting them to obey him no matter what he did—his family life was unstable, and his children never knew him well.

In many ways, then, my family's life reflects some of the contradictions of Kenya, and indeed, the African continent as a whole. The history of Africa is a history of ancient kingdoms and great traditions; the story of people fighting to be free from colonial rule; the heroism of not only of great men like Nkrumah and Kenyatta and Mandela, but also ordinary people who endured great hardship, from Ghana to South Africa, to secure self-determination in the face of great odds.

But for all the progress that has been made, we must surely acknowledge that neither Kenya nor the African continent have yet fulfilled their potential—that the hopefulness of the post-colonial era has been replaced by cynicism and sometimes despair, and that true freedom has not yet been won for those struggling to live on less than a few shillings a day, for those who have fallen prey to HIV/AIDS or malaria, to those ordinary citizens who continue to find themselves trapped in the crossfire of war or ethnic conflict.

One statistic powerfully describes this unfulfilled promise. In early 1960s, as Kenya was gaining its independence, its gross national product was not very different from that of South Korea. Today, South Korea's economy is forty times larger than Kenya's.

How can we explain this fact? Certainly it is not due to lack of effort on the part of ordinary Kenyans—we know how hard Kenyans are willing to work, the tremendous sacrifices that Kenyan mothers make for their children, the Herculean efforts that Kenyan fathers make for their families. We know as well the talent, the intelligence, and the creativity that exists in this country. And we know how much this land is blessed—just as the entire African continent is blessed—with great gifts and riches.

So what explains this? I believe there a number of factors at work.

Kenya, like many African nations did not come of age under the best historical circumstances. It suffers from the legacy of colonialism, of national boundaries that were drawn without regard to the political and tribal alignments of indigenous peoples, and that therefore fed conflict and tribal strife.

Kenya was also forced to rapidly move from a highly agrarian to a more urban, industrialized nation. This means that the education and health care systems—issues that my own nation more than 200 years old still struggles with—lag behind, impacting its development.

Third, Kenya is hurt from factors unique to Africa's geography and place in the world—disease, distance from viable markets, and especially terms of trade. When African nations were just gaining independence, industrialized nations had decades of experience building their domestic economies and navigating the international financial system. And, as Frederick Douglass once stated: "Power concedes nothing without a demand. It never did, and it never will." As a result, many African nations have been asked to liberalize their markets without reciprocal concessions from mature economies. This lack of access for Africa's agriculture and commodities has restricted an important engine of economic growth. Other issues, such as resource extraction and the drain of human capital have also been major factors.

As a senator from the United States, I believe that my country, and other nations, have an obligation and self-interest in being full partners with Kenya and with Africa. And, I will do my part to shape an intelligent foreign policy that promotes peace and prosperity. A foreign policy that gives hope and opportunity to the people of this great continent.

But, Kenya must do its part. It cannot wait for other nations to act first. The hard truth is that nations, by and large, will act in their self-interest and if Kenya does not act, it will fall behind.

It's more than just history and outside influences that explain why Kenya lags behind. Like many nations across this continent, where Kenya is failing is in its ability to create a government that is transparent and accountable. One that serves its people and is free from corruption.

There is no doubt that what Kenyans have accomplished with this independence is both impressive and inspiring. Among African nations, Kenya remains a model for representative democracy—a place where many different ethnic factions have found a way to live and work together in peace and stability. You enjoy a robust civil society; a press that's free, fair, and honest; and a strong partnership with my own country that has resulted in critical cooperation on terrorist issues, real strides in fighting disease and poverty, and an important alliance on fostering regional stability.

And yet, the reason I speak of the freedom that you fought so hard to win is because today that freedom is in jeopardy. It is being threatened by corruption.

Corruption is not a new problem. It's not just a Kenyan problem, or an African problem. It's a human problem, and it has existed in some form in almost every society. My own city of Chicago has been the home of some of the most corrupt local politics in American history, from patronage machines to questionable elections. In just the last year, our own U.S. Congress has seen a representative resign after taking bribes, and several others fall under investigation for using their public office for private gain.

But while corruption is a problem we all share, here in Kenya it is a crisis— a crisis that's robbing an honest people of the opportunities they have fought for—the opportunity they deserve.

I know that while recent reports have pointed to strong economic growth in this country, 56 percent of Kenyans still live in poverty. And I know that the vast majority of people in this country desperately want to change this.

It is painfully obvious that corruption stifles development—it siphons off scarce resources that could improve infrastructure, bolster education systems, and strengthen public health. It stacks the deck so high against entrepreneurs that they cannot get their job-creating ideas off the ground. In fact, one recent survey showed that corruption in Kenya costs local firms 6 percent of their revenues, the difference between good-paying jobs in Kenya or somewhere else. And corruption also erodes the state from the inside out, sickening the justice system until there is no justice to be found, poisoning the police forces until their presence becomes a source of insecurity rather than comfort.

Corruption has a way of magnifying the very worst twists of fate. It makes it impossible to respond effectively to crises—whether it's the HIV/AIDS pandemic or malaria or crippling drought.

What's worse—corruption can also provide opportunities for those who would harness the fear and hatred of others to their agenda and ambitions.

> "*In a true democracy, it is what happens between elections that is the true measure of how a government treats its people.*"

It can shield a war criminal—even one like Felicien Kabuga, suspected of helping to finance and orchestrate the Rwandan genocide—by allowing him to purchase safe haven for a time and robbing all humanity of the opportunity to bring the criminal to justice.

Terrorist attacks—like those that have shed Kenyan blood and struck at the heart of the Kenyan economy—are facilitated by customs and border officers who can be paid off, by police forces so crippled by corruption that they do not protect the personal safety of Kenyans walking the streets of Nairobi, and by forged documents that are easy to find in a climate where graft and fraud thrive.

Some of the worst actors on the international stage can also take advantage of the collective exhaustion and outrage that people feel with official corruption, as we've seen with Islamic extremists who promise purification, but deliver totalitarianism. Endemic corruption opens the door to this kind of movement, and in its wake comes a new set of distortions and betrayals of public trust.

In the end, if the people cannot trust their government to do the job for which it exists—to protect them and to promote their common welfare—all else is lost. And this is why the struggle against corruption is one of the great struggles of our time.

The good news is that there are already signs of progress here. Willingness to report corruption is increasing significantly in Kenya. The Kenyan media has been courageous in uncovering and reporting on some of the most blatant abuses of the system, and there has been a growing recognition among people and politicians that this is a critical issue.

Among other things, this recognition resulted in the coalition that came to power in the December elections of 2002. This coalition succeeded by promising change, and their early gestures— the dismissal of the shaky judges, the renewed vigor of the investigation into the Goldenberg scandal, the calls for real disclosure of elected officials' personal wealth—were all promising.

> *"Looking out at this crowd of young people, I have faith that you will fight this fight too."*

But elections are not enough. In a true democracy, it is what happens between elections that is the true measure of how a government treats its people.

Today, we're starting to see that the Kenyan people want more than a simple changing of the guard, more than piecemeal reforms to a crisis that's crippling their country. The Kenyan people are crying out for real change, and whether one voted orange or banana in last year's referendum, the message that many Kenyans seemed to be sending was one of dissatisfaction with the pace of reform, and real frustration with continued tolerance of corruption at high levels.

And so we know that there is more work to be done—more reforms to be made. I don't have all the solutions or think that they'll be easy, but there are a few places that a country truly committed to reform could start.

We know that the temptation to take a bribe is greater when you're not making enough on the job. And we also know that the more people there are on the government payroll, the more likely it is that someone will be encouraged to take a bribe. So if the government found ways to downsize the bureaucracy—

to cut out the positions that aren't necessary or useful—it could use the extra money to increase the salary of other government officials.

Of course, the best way to reduce bureaucracy and increase pay is to create more private sector jobs. And the way to create good jobs is when the rules of a society are transparent—when there's a clear and advertised set of laws and regulations regarding how to start a business, what it takes to own property, how to go about getting a loan—there is less of a chance that some corrupt bureaucrat will make up his own rules that suit only his interests. Clarifying these rules and focusing resources on building a judicial system that can enforce them and resolve disputes should be a primary goal of any government suffering from corruption.

In addition, we know that the more information the public is provided, the easier it will be for your Kenyan brothers and sisters out in the villages to evaluate whether they are being treated fairly by their public servants or not. Wealth declarations do little good if no one can access them, and accountability in government spending is not possible if no one knows how much was available and allocated to a given project in the first place.

Finally, ethnic-based tribal politics has to stop. It is rooted in the bankrupt idea that the goal of politics or business is to funnel as much of the pie as possible to one's family, tribe, or circle with little regard for the public good. It stifles innovation and fractures the fabric of the society. Instead of opening businesses and engaging in commerce, people come to rely on patronage and payback as a means of advancing. Instead of unifying the country to move forward on solving problems, it divides neighbor from neighbor.

An accountable, transparent government can break this cycle. When people are judged by merit, not connections, then the best and brightest can lead the country, people will work hard, and the entire economy will grow—everyone will benefit and more resources will be available for all, not just select groups.

Of course, in the end, one of the strongest weapons your country has against corruption is the ability of you, the people, to stand up and speak out about the injustices you see. The Kenyan people are the ultimate guardians against abuses.

The world knows the names of Wangari Maathai and John Githongo, who are fighting against the insidious corruption that has weakened Kenya. But there are so many others, some of whom I'm meeting during my visit here—Betty Murungi, Ken Njau, Jane Onyango, Maina Kiai, Milly Odhiombo, and Hussein Khalid. As well as numerous Kenyan men and women who have refused to pay bribes to get civil servants to perform their duties; the auditors and inspectors general who have done the job before them accurately and fairly, regardless of where the facts have led; the journalists who asked questions and pushed for answers when it may have been more lucrative to look the other way, or whip up a convenient fiction. And then there are anonymous Kenyan whistle-blowers who show us what is, so that we can all work together to demand what should be.

By rejecting the insulting idea that corruption is somehow a part of Kenyan culture, these heroes reveal the very opposite—they reveal a strength and integrity of character that can build a great country, a great future. By focusing on building strong, independent institutions—like an anti-corruption commission with real authority—rather than cults of personality, they make a contribution to their country that will last longer than their own lives. They fight the fight of our time.

Looking out at this crowd of young people, I have faith that you will fight this fight too.

You will decide if your leaders will be held accountable, or if you will look the other way.

You will decide if the standards and the rules will be the same for everyone—regardless of ethnicity or of wealth.

And you will determine the direction of this country in the 21st century—whether the hard work of the many is lost to the selfish desires of a few, or whether you build an open, honest, stronger Kenya where everyone rises together.

This is the Kenya that so many who came before you envisioned—all those men and women who struggled and sacrificed and fought for the freedom you enjoy today.

I know that honoring their memory and making that freedom real may seem like an impossible task—an effort bigger than you can imagine—but sometimes all it takes to move us there is doing what little you can to right the wrongs you see.

As I said at the outset, I did not know my father well—he returned to Kenya from America when I was still young. Since that time I have known him through stories—those my mother would tell and those I heard from my relatives here in Kenya on my last trip to this country.

I know from these stories that my father was not a perfect man—that he made his share of mistakes and disappointed his share of people in his lifetime.

As our parents' children, we have the opportunity to learn from these mistakes and disappointments. We have the opportunity to muster the courage to fulfill the promise of our forefathers and lead our great nations towards a better future.

In today's Kenya—a Kenya already more open and less repressive than in my father's day—it is that courage that will bring the reform so many of you so desperately want and deserve. I wish all of you luck in finding this courage in the days and months to come, and I want you to know that as your ally, your friend, and your brother, I will be there to help in any way I can. Thank you.

This Improbable Quest
Announcement for President
SPRINGFIELD, ILLINOIS • FEBRUARY 10, 2007

Let me begin by saying thanks to all you who've traveled, from far and wide, to brave the cold today.

We all made this journey for a reason. It's humbling, but in my heart I know you didn't come here just for me, you came here because you believe in what this

> "*Today we are called once more—and it is time for our generation to answer that call. For that is our unyielding faith—that in the face of impossible odds, people who love their country can change it.*"

country can be. In the face of war, you believe there can be peace. In the face of despair, you believe there can be hope. In the face of a politics that's shut you out, that's told you to settle, that's divided us for too long, you believe we can be one people, reaching for what's possible, building that more perfect union.

That's the journey we're on today. But let me tell you how I came to be here. As most of you know, I am not a native of this great state. I moved to Illinois over two decades ago. I was a young man then, just a year out of college; I knew no one in Chicago, was without money or family connections. But a group of churches had offered me a job as a community organizer for $13,000 a year. And I accepted the job, sight unseen, motivated then by a single, simple, powerful idea—that I might play a small part in building a better America.

My work took me to some of Chicago's poorest neighborhoods. I joined with pastors and lay-people to deal with communities that had been ravaged by plant closings. I saw that the problems people faced weren't simply local in nature—that the decision to close a steel mill was made by distant executives; that the lack of textbooks and computers in schools could be traced to the skewed priorities of politicians a thousand miles away; and that when a child turns to violence, there's a hole in his heart no government alone can fill.

It was in these neighborhoods that I received the best education I ever had, and where I learned the true meaning of my Christian faith.

After three years of this work, I went to law school, because I wanted to understand how the law should work for those in need. I became a civil rights lawyer, and taught constitutional law, and after a time, I came to understand that our cherished rights of liberty and equality depend on the active participation of an awakened electorate. It was with these ideas in mind that I arrived in this capital city as a state Senator.

It was here, in Springfield, where I saw all that is America converge—farmers and teachers, businessmen and laborers, all of them with a story to tell, all of them seeking a seat at the table, all of them clamoring to be heard. I made lasting friendships here—friends that I see in the audience today.

It was here we learned to disagree without being disagreeable—that it's possible to compromise so long as you know those principles that can never be compromised; and that so long as we're willing to listen to each other, we can assume the best in people instead of the worst.

That's why we were able to reform a death penalty system that was broken. That's why we were able to give health insurance to children in need. That's why we made the tax system more fair and just for working families, and that's why we passed ethics reforms that the cynics said could never, ever be passed.

It was here, in Springfield, where North, South, East, and West come together that I was reminded of the essential decency of the American people—where I came to believe that through this decency, we can build a more hopeful America.

And that is why, in the shadow of the Old State Capitol, where Lincoln once called on a divided house to stand together, where common hopes and common dreams still, I stand before you today to announce my candidacy for President of the United States.

I recognize there is a certain presumptuousness—a certain audacity—to this announcement. I know I haven't spent a lot of time learning the ways of Washington. But I've been there long enough to know that the ways of Washington must change.

The genius of our founders is that they designed a system of government that can be changed. And we should take heart, because we've changed this country before. In the face of tyranny, a band of patriots brought an Empire to its knees. In the face of secession, we unified a nation and set the captives free. In the face of Depression, we put people back to work and lifted millions out of poverty.

We welcomed immigrants to our shores, we opened railroads to the west, we landed a man on the moon, and we heard a King's call to let justice roll down like water, and righteousness like a mighty stream.

Each and every time, a new generation has risen up and done what's needed to be done. Today we are called once more—and it is time for our generation to answer that call.

For that is our unyielding faith—that in the face of impossible odds, people who love their country can change it.

That's what Abraham Lincoln understood. He had his doubts. He had his defeats. He had his setbacks. But through his will and his words, he moved a nation and helped free a people. It is because of the millions who rallied to his cause that we are no longer divided, North and South, slave and free. It is because men and women of every race, from every walk of life, continued to march for freedom long after Lincoln was laid to rest, that today we have the chance to face the challenges of this millennium together, as one people—as Americans.

All of us know what those challenges are today—a war with no end, a dependence on oil that threatens our future, schools where too many children aren't learning, and families struggling paycheck to paycheck despite working as hard as they can. We know the challenges. We've heard them. We've talked about them for years.

What's stopped us from meeting these challenges is not the absence of sound policies and sensible plans. What's stopped us is the failure of leadership, the smallness of our politics—the ease with which we're distracted by the petty and trivial, our chronic avoidance of tough decisions, our preference for scoring cheap political points instead of rolling up our sleeves and building a working consensus to tackle big problems.

For the last six years we've been told that our mounting debts don't matter, we've been told that the anxiety Americans feel about rising health care costs and stagnant wages are an illusion, we've been told that climate change is a hoax, and that tough talk and an ill-conceived war can replace diplomacy, and strategy, and foresight. And when all else fails, when Katrina happens, or the death toll in Iraq mounts, we've been told that our crises are somebody else's fault. We're distracted from our real failures, and told to blame the other party, or gay people, or immigrants.

And as people have looked away in disillusionment and frustration, we know what's filled the void. The cynics, and the lobbyists, and the special interests who've turned our government into a game only they can afford to play.

> *"We can turn this crisis of global warming into a moment of opportunity for innovation, and job creation, and an incentive for businesses that will serve as a model for the world."*

They write the checks and you get stuck with the bills, they get the access while you get to write a letter, they think they own this government, but we're here today to take it back. The time for that politics is over. It's time to turn the page.

We've made some progress already. I was proud to help lead the fight in Congress that led to the most sweeping ethics reform since Watergate.

But Washington has a long way to go. And it won't be easy. That's why we'll have to set priorities. We'll have to make hard choices. And although government will play a crucial role in bringing about the changes we need, more money and programs alone will not get us where we need to go. Each of us, in our own lives, will have to accept responsibility—for instilling an ethic of achievement in our children, for adapting to a more competitive economy, for strengthening our communities, and sharing some measure of sacrifice. So let us begin. Let us begin this hard work together. Let us transform this nation.

Let us be the generation that reshapes our economy to compete in the digital age. Let's set high standards for our schools and give them the resources they need to succeed. Let's recruit a new army of teachers, and give them better pay and more support in exchange for more accountability. Let's make college more affordable, and let's invest in scientific research, and let's lay down broadband lines through the heart of inner cities and rural towns all across America.

And as our economy changes, let's be the generation that ensures our nation's workers are sharing in our prosperity. Let's protect the hard-earned benefits their companies have promised. Let's make it possible for hardworking Americans to save for retirement. And let's allow our unions and their organizers to lift up this country's middle-class again.

Let's be the generation that ends poverty in America. Every single person willing to work should be able to get job training that leads to a job, and earn a living wage that can pay the bills, and afford child care so their kids have a safe place to go when they work. Let's do this.

> " *That is why this campaign can't only be about me. It must be about us— it must be about what we can do together.* "

Let's be the generation that finally tackles our health care crisis. We can control costs by focusing on prevention, by providing better treatment to the chronically ill, and using technology to cut the bureaucracy. Let's be the generation that says right here, right now, that we will have universal health care in America by the end of the next president's first term.

Let's be the generation that finally frees America from the tyranny of oil. We can harness homegrown, alternative fuels like ethanol and spur the production of more fuel-efficient cars. We can set up a system for capping greenhouse gases. We can turn this crisis of global warming into a moment of opportunity for innovation, and job creation, and an incentive for businesses that will serve as a model for the world. Let's be the generation that makes future generations proud of what we did here.

Most of all, let's be the generation that never forgets what happened on that September day and confront the terrorists with everything we've got. Politics doesn't have to divide us on this anymore—we can work together to keep our country safe. I've worked with Republican Senator Dick Lugar to pass a law that will secure and destroy some of the world's deadliest, unguarded weapons. We can work together to track terrorists down with a stronger military, we can tighten the net around their finances, and we can improve our intelligence capabilities. But let us also understand that ultimate victory against our enemies will come only by rebuilding our alliances and exporting those ideals that bring hope and opportunity to millions around the globe.

But all of this cannot come to pass until we bring an end to this war in Iraq. Most of you know I opposed this war from the start. I thought it was a tragic mistake. Today we grieve for the families who have lost loved ones, the hearts that have been broken, and the young lives that could have been. America, it's time to start bringing our troops home. It's time to admit that no amount of American lives can resolve the political disagreement that lies at the heart of someone else's civil war. That's why I have a plan that will bring our combat troops home by March of 2008. Letting the Iraqis know that we will not be there forever is our last, best hope to pressure the Sunni and Shia to come to the table and find peace.

Finally, there is one other thing that is not too late to get right about this war—and that is the homecoming of the men and women—our veterans—who have sacrificed the most. Let us honor their valor by providing the care they need and rebuilding the military they love. Let us be the generation that begins this work.

I know there are those who don't believe we can do all these things. I understand the skepticism. After all, every four years, candidates from both parties make similar promises, and I expect this year will be no different. All of us running for president will travel around the country offering ten-point plans and making grand speeches; all of us will trumpet those qualities we believe make us uniquely qualified to lead the country. But too many times, after the election is over, and the confetti is swept away, all those promises fade from memory, and the lobbyists and the special interests move in, and people turn away, disappointed as before, left to struggle on their own.

That is why this campaign can't only be about me. It must be about us—it must be about what we can do together. This campaign must be the occasion, the vehicle, of your hopes, and your dreams. It will take your time, your energy, and your advice—to push us forward when we're doing right, and to let us know when we're not. This campaign has to be about reclaiming the meaning of citizenship, restoring our sense of common purpose, and realizing that few obstacles can withstand the power of millions of voices calling for change.

By ourselves, this change will not happen. Divided, we are bound to fail.

But the life of a tall, gangly, self-made Springfield lawyer tells us that a different future is possible.

He tells us that there is power in words.

He tells us that there is power in conviction.

That beneath all the differences of race and region, faith and station, we are one people.

He tells us that there is power in hope.

As Lincoln organized the forces arrayed against slavery, he was heard to say: "Of strange, discordant, and even hostile elements, we gathered from the four winds, and formed and fought to battle through."

That is our purpose here today.

That's why I'm in this race.

Not just to hold an office, but to gather with you to transform a nation.

I want to win that next battle—for justice and opportunity.

I want to win that next battle—for better schools, and better jobs, and health care for all.

I want us to take up the unfinished business of perfecting our union, and building a better America.

And if you will join me in this improbable quest, if you feel destiny calling, and see as I see, a future of endless possibility stretching before us; if you sense, as I sense, that the time is now to shake off our slumber, and slough off our fear, and make good on the debt we owe past and future generations, then I'm ready to take up the cause, and march with you, and work with you. Together, starting today, let us finish the work that needs to be done, and usher in a new birth of freedom on this earth.

Reach for What We Know Is Possible

Remarks at the Iowa Jefferson-Jackson Dinner

DES MOINES, IOWA • NOVEMBER 10, 2007

Thank you so much. To the great Governor of Iowa and Lieutenant Governor of Iowa. To my dear friend Tom Harkin for the outstanding work that he does. To the congressional delegation of Iowa that is doing outstanding work and to Nancy Pelosi, Madam Speaker, thank you all for the wonderful welcome and the wonderful hospitality.

A little less than one year from today, you will go into the voting booth and you will select the President of the United States of America.

Now, here's the good news—the name George W. Bush will not be on the ballot. The name of my cousin Dick Cheney will not be on the ballot. We've been trying to hide that for a long time. Everybody has a black sheep in the family. The era of Scooter Libby justice, and Brownie incompetence, and Karl Rove politics will finally be over.

But the question you're going to have to ask yourself when you caucus in January and you vote in November is, "What's next for America?"

We are in a defining moment in our history. Our nation is at war. The planet is in peril. The dream that so

> **"And I will send once more a message to those yearning faces beyond our shores that says, 'You matter to us. Your future is our future. And our moment is now.'"**

many generations fought for feels as if it's slowly slipping away. We are working harder for less. We've never paid more for health care or for college. It's harder to save and it's harder to retire. And most of all we've lost faith that our leaders can or will do anything about it.

We were promised compassionate conservatism and all we got was Katrina and wiretaps. We were promised a uniter, and we got a president who could not even lead the half of the country that voted for him. We were promised a more ethical and more efficient government, and instead we have a town called Washington that is more corrupt and more wasteful than it was before. And the only mission that was ever accomplished is to use fear and falsehood to take this country to a war that should have never been authorized and should have never been waged.

It is because of these failures that America is listening, intently, to what we say here today—not just Democrats, but Republicans and Independents who've lost trust in their government, but want to believe again.

And it is because of these failures that we not only have a moment of great challenge, but also a moment of great opportunity. We have a chance to bring the country together in a new majority—to finally tackle problems that George Bush made far worse, but that had festered long before George Bush ever took office—problems that we've talked about year after year after year after year.

And that is why the same old Washington textbook campaigns just won't do in this election. That's why not answering questions 'cause we are afraid our answers won't be popular just won't do. That's why telling the American people what we think they want to hear instead of telling the American people what they need to hear just won't do. Triangulating and poll-driven positions because we're worried about what Mitt or Rudy might say about us just won't do. If we are really serious about wining this election Democrats, we can't live in fear of losing it.

This party—the party of Jefferson and Jackson; of Roosevelt and Kennedy—has always made the biggest difference in the lives of the American people when we led not by polls, but by principle; not by calculation, but by conviction; when we summoned the entire nation to a common purpose—a higher purpose. And I run for the Presidency of the United States of America because that's the party America needs us to be right now.

A party that offers not just a difference in policies, but a difference in leadership.

A party that doesn't just focus on how to win but why we should.

A party that doesn't just offer change as a slogan, but real, meaningful change—change that America can believe in.

That's why I'm in this race. That's why I am running for the presidency of the United States of America—to offer change that we can believe in.

I am in this race to tell the corporate lobbyists that their days of setting the agenda in Washington are over. I

> "*I am running in this race because of what Dr. King called 'the fierce urgency of now.' Because I believe that there's such a thing as being too late. And that hour is almost upon us.*"

have done more than any other candidate in this race to take on lobbyists—and won. They have not funded my campaign, they will not get a job in my White House, and they will not drown out the voices of the American people when I am president.

I'm in this race to take those tax breaks away from companies that are moving jobs overseas and put them in the pockets of hard working Americans who deserve it. And I won't raise the minimum wage every ten years—I will raise it to keep pace so that workers don't fall behind.

That is why I am in it. To protect the American worker. To fight for the American worker.

I'm in this race because I want to stop talking about the outrage of 47 million Americans without health care and start actually doing something about it. I expanded health care in Illinois by bringing Democrats and Republicans together. By taking on the insurance industry. And that is how I will make certain that every single American in this country has health care they can count on and I won't do it twenty years from now, I won't do it ten years from now, I will do it by the end of my first term as President of the United States of America.

I run for president to make sure that every American child has the best education that we have to offer—from the day they are born to the day they graduate from college. And I won't just talk about how great teachers are—as president I will reward them for their greatness—by raising salaries and giving them more support. That's why I'm in this race.

I am running for president because I am sick and tired of Democrats thinking that the only way to look tough on national security is by talking, and acting, and voting like George Bush Republicans.

When I am this party's nominee, my opponent will not be able to say that I voted for the war in Iraq; or that I gave George Bush the benefit of the doubt on Iran; or that I supported Bush-Cheney policies of not talking to leaders that we don't like. And he will not be able to say that I wavered on something as fundamental as whether or not it is ok for America to torture—because it is never ok. That's why I am in it.

As president, I will end the war in Iraq. We will have our troops home in sixteen months. I will close Guantanamo. I will restore habeas corpus. I will finish the fight against Al Qaeda. And I will lead the world to combat the common threats of the 21st century—nuclear weapons and terrorism; climate change and poverty; genocide and disease. And I will send once more a message to those yearning faces beyond our shores that says, "You matter to us. Your future is our future. And our moment is now."

America, our moment is now.

Our moment is now.

I don't want to spend the next year or the next four years re-fighting the same fights that we had in the 1990s.

I don't want to pit Red America against Blue America, I want to be the President of the United States of America.

And if those Republicans come at me with the same fear-mongering and swift-boating that they usually do, then I will take them head on. Because I believe the American people are tired of fear and tired of distractions and tired of diversions. We can make this election not about fear, but about the future. And that won't just be a Democratic victory; that will be an American victory.

And that is a victory America needs right now.

I am not in this race to fulfill some long-held ambitions or because I believe it's somehow owed to me. I never expected to be here, I always knew this journey was improbable. I've never been on a journey that wasn't.

I am running in this race because of what Dr. King called "the fierce urgency of now." Because I believe that there's such a thing as being too late. And that hour is almost upon us.

I don't want to wake up four years from now and find out that millions of Americans still lack health care because we couldn't take on the insurance industry.

I don't want to see that the oceans have risen a few more inches. The planet has reached a point of no return because we couldn't find a way to stop buying oil from dictators.

I don't want to see more American lives put at risk because no one had the judgment or the courage to stand up against a misguided war before we sent our troops in to fight.

I don't want to see homeless veterans on the streets. I don't want to send another generation of American children to failing schools. I don't want that future for my daughters. I don't want that future for your sons. I do not want that future for America.

I'm in this race for the same reason that I fought for jobs for the jobless and hope for the hopeless on the streets of Chicago; for the same reason I fought for justice and equality as a civil rights lawyer; for the same reason that I fought for Illinois families for over a decade.

Because I will never forget that the only reason that I'm standing here today is because somebody, somewhere stood up for me when it was risky. Stood up when it was hard. Stood up when it wasn't popular. And because that somebody stood up, a few more stood up. And then a few thousand stood up. And then a few million stood up. And standing up, with courage and clear purpose, they somehow managed to change the world.

That's why I'm running, Iowa—to give our children and grandchildren the same chances somebody gave me.

That's why I'm running, Democrats—to keep the American Dream alive for those who still hunger for opportunity, who still thirst for equality.

That's why I'm asking you to stand with me, that's why I'm asking you to caucus for me, that's why I am asking you to stop settling for what the cynics say we have to accept. In this election—in this moment—let us reach for what we know is possible. A nation healed. A world repaired. An America that believes again. Thank you very much everybody.

Our Time for Change Has Come

Iowa Caucus Night

DES MOINES, IOWA • JANUARY 3, 2008

Thank you, Iowa.

You know, they said this day would never come.

They said our sights were set too high.

They said this country was too divided; too disillusioned to ever come together around a common purpose.

But on this January night—at this defining moment in history—you have done what the cynics said we couldn't do. You have done what the state of New Hampshire can do in five days. You have done what America can do in this New Year, 2008. In lines that stretched around schools and churches; in small towns and big cities; you came together as Democrats, Republicans, and Independents to stand up and say that we are one nation; we are one people; and our time for change has come.

You said the time has come to move beyond the bitterness and pettiness and anger that's consumed Washington; to end the political strategy that's been all about division and instead make it about addition—to build a coalition for change that stretches through Red States and Blue States. Because that's how we'll win in November, and that's how we'll finally meet the challenges that we face as a nation.

We are choosing hope over fear. We're choosing unity over division, and sending a powerful message that change is coming to America.

You said the time has come to tell the lobbyists who think their money and their influence speak louder than our voices that they don't own this government, we do; and we are here to take it back.

The time has come for a president who will be honest about the choices and the challenges we face; who will listen to you and learn from you even when we disagree; who won't just tell you what you want to hear, but what you need to know. And in New Hampshire, if you give me the same chance that Iowa did tonight, I will be that president for America.

> *"On this January night—at this defining moment in history—you have done what the cynics said we couldn't do."*

I'll be a president who finally makes health care affordable and available to every single American the same way I expanded health care in Illinois—by bringing Democrats and Republicans together to get the job done.

I'll be a president who ends the tax breaks for companies that ship our jobs overseas and put a middle-class tax cut into the pockets of the working Americans who deserve it.

I'll be a president who harnesses the ingenuity of farmers and scientists and entrepreneurs to free this nation from the tyranny of oil once and for all.

And I'll be a president who ends this war in Iraq and finally brings our troops home; who restores our moral standing; who understands that 9/11 is not a way to scare up votes, but a challenge that should unite America and the world against the common threats of the 21st century; common threats of terrorism and nuclear weapons; climate change and poverty; genocide and disease.

Tonight, we are one step closer to that vision of America because of what you did here in Iowa. And so I'd especially like to thank the organizers and the precinct captains; the volunteers and the staff who made this all possible.

And while I'm at it, on "thank yous," I think it makes sense for me to thank the love of my life, the rock of the Obama family, the closer on the campaign trail; give it up for Michelle Obama.

I know you didn't do this for me. You did this—you did this because you believed so deeply in the most American of ideas—that in the face of impossible odds, people who love this country can change it.

> *"Years from now, you'll look back and you'll say that this was the moment—this was the place—where America remembered what it means to hope."*

I know this—I know this because while I may be standing here tonight, I'll never forget that my journey began on the streets of Chicago doing what so many of you have done for this campaign and all the campaigns here in Iowa—organizing, and working, and fighting to make people's lives just a little bit better.

I know how hard it is. It comes with little sleep, little pay, and a lot of sacrifice. There are days of disappointment, but sometimes, just sometimes, there are nights like this—a night—a night that, years from now, when we've made the changes we believe in; when more families can afford to see a doctor; when our children—when Malia and Sasha and your children—inherit a planet that's a little cleaner and safer; when the world sees America differently, and America sees itself as a nation less divided and more united; you'll be able to look back with pride and say that this was the moment when it all began.

This was the moment when the improbable beat what Washington always said was inevitable.

This was the moment when we tore down barriers that have divided us for too long—when we rallied people of all parties and ages to a common cause;

when we finally gave Americans who'd never participated in politics a reason to stand up and to do so.

This was the moment when we finally beat back the politics of fear, and doubt, and cynicism; the politics where we tear each other down instead of lifting this country up. This was the moment.

Years from now, you'll look back and you'll say that this was the moment—this was the place—where America remembered what it means to hope.

For many months, we've been teased, even derided for talking about hope.

But we always knew that hope is not blind optimism. It's not ignoring the enormity of the task ahead or the roadblocks that stand in our path. It's not sitting on the sidelines or shirking from a fight. Hope is that thing inside us that insists, despite all evidence to the contrary, that something better awaits us if we have the courage to reach for it, and to work for it, and to fight for it.

Hope is what I saw in the eyes of the young woman in Cedar Rapids who works the night shift after a full day of college and still can't afford health care for a sister who's ill; a young woman who still believes that this country will give her the chance to live out her dreams.

Hope is what I heard in the voice of the New Hampshire woman who told me that she hasn't been able to breathe since her nephew left for Iraq; who still goes to bed each night praying for his safe return.

Hope is what led a band of colonists to rise up against an empire; what led the greatest of generations to free a continent and heal a nation; what led young women and young men to sit at lunch counters and brave fire hoses and march through Selma and Montgomery for freedom's cause.

Hope is what led me here today—with a father from Kenya; a mother from Kansas; and a story that could only happen in the United States of America. Hope is the bedrock of this nation; the belief that our destiny will not be written for us, but by us; by all those men and women who are not content to settle for the world as it is; who have the courage to remake the world as it should be.

That is what we started here in Iowa, and that is the message we can now carry to New Hampshire and beyond; the same message we had when we were up and when we were down; the one that can change this country brick by brick, block by block, calloused hand by calloused hand—that together, ordinary people can do extraordinary things; because we are not a collection of Red States and Blue States, we are the United States of America; and at this moment, in this election, we are ready to believe again. Thank you, Iowa.

Yes We Can

New Hampshire Primary Concession Speech

NASHUA, NEW HAMPSHIRE • JANUARY 8, 2008

I want to congratulate Senator Clinton on a hard-fought victory here in New Hampshire.

A few weeks ago, no one imagined that we'd have accomplished what we did here tonight. For most of this campaign, we were far behind, and we always knew our climb would be steep.

But in record numbers, you came out and spoke up for change. And with your voices and your votes, you made it clear that at this moment—in this election—there is something happening in America.

There is something happening when men and women in Des Moines and Davenport; in Lebanon and Concord come out in the snows of January to wait in lines that stretch block after block because they believe in what this country can be.

There is something happening when Americans who are young in age and in spirit—who have never before participated in politics—turn out in numbers we've never seen because they know in their hearts that this time must be different.

There is something happening when people vote not just for the party they belong to but the hopes they hold in common—that whether we are rich or poor;

black or white; Latino or Asian; whether we hail from Iowa or New Hampshire, Nevada or South Carolina, we are ready to take this country in a fundamentally new direction. That is what's happening in America right now. Change is what's happening in America.

You can be the new majority who can lead this nation out of a long political darkness—Democrats, Independents, and Republicans who are tired of the division and distraction that has clouded Washington; who know that we can disagree without being disagreeable; who understand that if we mobilize our voices to challenge the money and influence that's stood in our way and challenge ourselves to reach for something better, there's no problem we can't solve—no destiny we cannot fulfill.

"We know the battle ahead will be long, but always remember that no matter what obstacles stand in our way, nothing can withstand the power of millions of voices calling for change."

Our new American majority can end the outrage of unaffordable, unavailable health care in our time. We can bring doctors and patients; workers and businesses, Democrats and Republicans together; and we can tell the drug and insurance industry that while they'll get a seat at the table, they don't get to buy every chair. Not this time. Not now.

Our new majority can end the tax breaks for corporations that ship our jobs overseas and put a middle-class tax cut into the pockets of the working Americans who deserve it.

We can stop sending our children to schools with corridors of shame and start putting them on a pathway to success. We can stop talking about how great teachers are and start rewarding them for their greatness. We can do this with our new majority.

We can harness the ingenuity of farmers and scientists; citizens and entrepreneurs to free this nation from the tyranny of oil and save our planet from a point of no return.

And when I am president, we will end this war in Iraq and bring our troops home; we will finish the job against al Qaeda in Afghanistan; we will care for our veterans; we will restore our moral standing in the world; and we will never use 9/11 as a way to scare up votes, because it is not a tactic to win an election, it is a challenge that should unite America and the world against the common threats of the 21st century: terrorism and nuclear weapons; climate change and poverty; genocide and disease.

> *"It was the call of workers who organized; women who reached for the ballot; a president who chose the moon as our new frontier; and a King who took us to the mountaintop and pointed the way to the Promised Land."*

All of the candidates in this race share these goals. All have good ideas. And all are patriots who serve this country honorably.

But the reason our campaign has always been different is because it's not just about what I will do as president, it's also about what you, the people who love this country, can do to change it.

That's why tonight belongs to you. It belongs to the organizers and the volunteers and the staff who believed in our improbable journey and rallied so many others to join.

We know the battle ahead will be long, but always remember that no matter what obstacles stand in our way, nothing can withstand the power of millions of voices calling for change.

We have been told we cannot do this by a chorus of cynics who will only grow louder and more dissonant in the weeks to come. We've been asked to pause for a reality check. We've been warned against offering the people of this nation false hope.

But in the unlikely story that is America, there has never been anything false about hope. For when we have faced down impossible odds; when we've been told that we're not ready, or that we shouldn't try, or that we can't, generations of Americans have responded with a simple creed that sums up the spirit of a people.

Yes we can.

It was a creed written into the founding documents that declared the destiny of a nation.

Yes we can.

It was whispered by slaves and abolitionists as they blazed a trail toward freedom through the darkest of nights.

Yes we can.

It was sung by immigrants as they struck out from distant shores and pioneers who pushed westward against an unforgiving wilderness.

Yes we can.

It was the call of workers who organized; women who reached for the ballot; a president who chose the moon as our new frontier; and a King who took us to the mountaintop and pointed the way to the Promised Land.

Yes we can, to justice and equality. Yes we can, to opportunity and prosperity. Yes we can heal this nation. Yes we can repair this world. Yes we can.

And so tomorrow, as we take this campaign South and West; as we learn that the struggles of the textile worker in Spartanburg are not so different than the plight of the dishwasher in Las Vegas; that the hopes of the little girl who goes to a crumbling school in Dillon are the same as the dreams of the boy who learns on the streets of L.A.; we will remember that there is something happening in America; that we are not as divided as our politics suggests; that we are one people; we are one nation; and together, we will begin the next great chapter in America's story with three words that will ring from coast to coast; from sea to shining sea—Yes. We. Can.

Ready to Believe Again

South Carolina Primary Victory Speech

COLUMBIA, SOUTH CAROLINA • JANUARY 26, 2008

Over two weeks ago, we saw the people of Iowa proclaim that our time for change has come. But there were those who doubted this country's desire for something new—who said Iowa was a fluke not to be repeated again.

Well, tonight, the cynics who believed that what began in the snows of Iowa was just an illusion were told a different story by the good people of South Carolina.

After four great contests in every corner of this country, we have the most votes, the most delegates, and the most diverse coalition of Americans we've seen in a long, long time.

They are young and old; rich and poor. They are black and white; Latino and Asian. They are Democrats from Des Moines and Independents from Concord; Republicans from rural Nevada and young people across this country who've never had a reason to participate until now. And in nine days, nearly half the nation will have the chance to join us in saying that we are tired of business-as-usual in Washington, we are hungry for change, and we are ready to believe again

But if there's anything we've been reminded of since Iowa, it's that the kind of change we seek will not come easy. Partly because we have fine candidates in the field—fierce competitors, worthy of respect. And as contentious as this campaign may get, we have to remember that this is a contest for the Democratic nomination, and that all of us share an abiding desire to end the disastrous policies of the current administration.

But there are real differences between the candidates. We are looking for more than just a change of party in the White House. We're looking to fundamentally change the status quo in Washington—a status quo that extends beyond any particular party. And right now, that status quo is fighting back with everything it's got; with the same old tactics that divide and distract us from solving the problems people face, whether those problems are health care they can't afford or a mortgage they cannot pay.

So this will not be easy. Make no mistake about what we're up against.

We are up against the belief that it's ok for lobbyists to dominate our government—that they are just part of the system in Washington. But we know that the undue influence of lobbyists is part of the problem, and this election is our chance to say that we're not going to let them stand in our way anymore.

We are up against the conventional thinking that says your ability to lead as president comes from longevity in Washington or proximity to the White House. But we know that real leadership is about candor, and judgment, and the ability to rally Americans from all walks of life around a common purpose—a higher purpose.

We are up against decades of bitter partisanship that cause politicians to demonize their opponents instead of coming together to make college affordable or energy cleaner; it's the kind of partisanship where you're not even allowed to say that a Republican had an idea—even if it's one you never agreed with. That kind of politics is bad for our party, it's bad for our country, and this is our chance to end it once and for all.

We are up against the idea that it's acceptable to say anything and do anything to win an election. We know that this is exactly what's wrong with our politics; this is why people don't

"The choice in this election is not between regions or religions or genders. It's not about rich versus poor; young versus old; and it is not about black versus white. It's about the past versus the future."

believe what their leaders say anymore; this is why they tune out. And this election is our chance to give the American people a reason to believe again.

And what we've seen in these last weeks is that we're also up against forces that are not the fault of any one campaign, but feed the habits that prevent us from being who we want to be as a nation. It's the politics that uses religion as a wedge, and patriotism as a bludgeon. A politics that tells us that we have to think, act, and even vote within the confines of the categories that supposedly define us. The assumption that young people are apathetic. The assumption that Republicans won't cross over. The assumption that the wealthy care nothing for the poor, and that the poor don't vote. The assumption that African-Americans can't support the white candidate; whites can't support the African-American candidate; blacks and Latinos can't come together.

But we are here tonight to say that this is not the America we believe in. I did not travel around this state over the last year and see a white South Carolina or a black South Carolina. I saw South Carolina. I saw crumbling schools that are stealing the future of black children and white children. I saw shuttered mills and homes for sale that once belonged to Americans from all walks of life, and men and women of every color and creed who serve together, and fight together, and bleed together under the same proud flag. I saw what America is, and I believe in what this country can be.

That is the country I see. That is the country you see. But now it is up to us to help the entire nation embrace this vision. Because in the end, we are not just up against the ingrained and destructive habits of Washington, we are also struggling against our own doubts, our own fears, and our own cynicism. The change we seek has always required great struggle and sacrifice. And so this is a battle in our own hearts and minds about what kind of country we want and how hard we're willing to work for it.

So let me remind you tonight that change will not be easy. That change will take time. There will be setbacks, and false starts, and sometimes we will make mistakes. But as hard as it may seem, we cannot lose hope. Because there are people all across this country who are counting us; who can't afford another four years without health care or good schools or decent wages because our leaders couldn't come together and get it done.

Theirs are the stories and voices we carry on from South Carolina.

The mother who can't get Medicaid to cover all the needs of her sick child—she needs us to pass a health care plan that cuts costs and makes health care available and affordable for every single American.

The teacher who works another shift at Dunkin' Donuts after school just to make ends meet—she needs us to reform our education system so that she gets better pay, and more support, and her students get the resources they need to achieve their dreams.

The Maytag worker who is now competing with his own teenager for a $7-an-hour job at Wal-Mart because the factory he gave his life to shut its doors—he needs us to stop giving tax breaks to companies that ship our jobs overseas and start putting them in the pockets of working Americans who deserve it. And struggling homeowners. And seniors who should retire with dignity and respect.

The woman who told me that she hasn't been able to breathe since the day her nephew left for Iraq, or the soldier who doesn't know his child because he's on his third or fourth tour of duty—they need us to come together and put an end to a war that should've never been authorized and never been waged.

The choice in this election is not between regions or religions or genders. It's not about rich versus poor; young versus old; and it is not about black versus white.

It's about the past versus the future.

It's about whether we settle for the same divisions and distractions and drama that passes for politics today, or whether we reach for a politics of common sense, and innovation—a shared sacrifice and shared prosperity.

There are those who will continue to tell us we cannot do this. That we cannot have what we long for. That we are peddling false hopes.

But here's what I know. I know that when people say we can't overcome all the big money and influence in Washington, I think of the elderly woman who sent me a contribution the other day—an envelope that had a money order for $3.01 along with a verse of scripture tucked inside. So don't tell us change isn't possible.

When I hear the cynical talk that blacks and whites and Latinos can't join together and work together, I'm reminded of the Latino brothers and sisters I organized with, and stood with, and fought with side by side for jobs and justice on the streets of Chicago. So don't tell us change can't happen.

When I hear that we'll never overcome the racial divide in our politics, I think about that Republican woman who used to work for Strom Thurmond, who's now devoted to educating inner-city children and who went out onto the streets of South Carolina and knocked on doors for this campaign. Don't tell me we can't change.

Yes we can change.

Yes we can heal this nation.

Yes we can seize our future.

And as we leave this state with a new wind at our backs, and take this journey across the country we love with the message we've carried from the plains of Iowa to the hills of New Hampshire; from the Nevada desert to the South Carolina coast; the same message we had when we were up and when we were down—that out of many, we are one; that while we breathe, we hope; and where we are met with cynicism, and doubt, and those who tell us that we can't, we will respond with that timeless creed that sums up the spirit of a people in three simple words: Yes. We. Can.

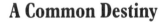

A Common Destiny

Potomac Primary Victory Speech

Madison, Wisconsin • February 12, 2008

Today, the change we seek swept through the Chesapeake and over the Potomac.

We won the state of Maryland. We won the Commonwealth of Virginia. And though we won in Washington, D.C., this movement won't stop until there's change in Washington. And tonight, we're on our way.

But we know how much farther we have to go.

We know it takes more than one night—or even one election—to overcome decades of money and the influence; bitter partisanship and petty bickering that's shut you out, let you down and told you to settle.

> " *This is the new American majority. This is what change looks like when it happens from the bottom up. And in this election, your voices will be heard.* "

We know our road will not be easy.

But we also know that at this moment the cynics can no longer say our hope is false.

We have now won east and west, north and south, and across the heartland of this country we love. We have given young people a reason to believe, and brought folks back to the polls who want to believe again. And we are bringing together Democrats and Independents and Republicans; blacks and whites; Latinos and Asians; small states and big states; Red States and Blue States into a United States of America.

This is the new American majority. This is what change looks like when it happens from the bottom up. And in this election, your voices will be heard.

Because at a time when so many people are struggling to keep up with soaring costs in a sluggish economy, we know that the status quo in Washington just won't do. Not this time. Not this year. We can't keep playing the same Washington game with the same Washington players and expect a different result—because it's a game that ordinary Americans are losing.

It's a game where lobbyists write check after check and Exxon turns record profits, while you pay the price at the pump, and our planet is put at risk. That's what happens when lobbyists set the agenda, and that's why they won't drown out your voices anymore when I am president of the United States of America.

It's a game where trade deals like NAFTA ship jobs overseas and force parents to compete with their teenagers to work for minimum wage at Wal-Mart. That's what happens when the American worker doesn't have a voice at the negotiating table, when leaders change their positions on trade with the politics of the moment, and that's why we need a president who will listen to Main Street—not just Wall Street; a president who will stand with workers not just when it's easy, but when it's hard.

It's a game where Democrats and Republicans fail to come together year after year after year, while another mother goes without health care for her sick child. That's why we have to put an end to the division and distraction in Washington, so that we can unite this nation around a common purpose, a higher purpose.

> " *The voices of the American people have carried us a great distance on this improbable journey, but we have much further to go.* "

It's a game where the only way for Democrats to look tough on national security is by talking, and acting, and voting like Bush-McCain Republicans, while our troops are sent to fight tour after tour of duty in a war that should've never been authorized and should've never been waged. That's what happens when we use 9/11 to scare up votes, and that's why we need to do more than end a war—we need to end the mindset that got us into war.

That's the choice in this primary. It's about whether we choose to play the game, or whether we choose to end it; it's change that polls well, or change we can believe in; it's the past versus the future. And when I'm the Democratic nominee for president—that will be the choice in November.

John McCain is an American hero. We honor his service to our nation. But his priorities don't address the real problems of the American people, because they are bound to the failed policies of the past.

George Bush won't be on the ballot this November, but his war and his tax cuts for the wealthy will.

When I am the nominee, I will offer a clear choice. John McCain won't be able to say that I ever supported this war in Iraq, because I opposed it from the beginning. Senator McCain said the other day that we might be mired for a hundred years in Iraq, which is reason enough to not give him four years in the White House.

If we had chosen a different path, the right path, we could have finished the job in Afghanistan, and put more resources into the fight against bin Laden; and instead of spending hundreds of billions of dollars in Baghdad, we could have put that money into our schools and hospitals, our roads and bridges—and that's what the American people need us to do right now.

And I admired Senator McCain when he stood up and said that it offended his "conscience" to support the Bush tax cuts for the wealthy in a time of war; that he couldn't support a tax cut where "so many of the benefits go to the most fortunate." But somewhere along the road to the Republican nomination, the Straight Talk Express lost its wheels, because now he's all for them.

Well I'm not. We can't keep spending money that we don't have in a war that we shouldn't have fought. We can't keep mortgaging our children's future on a mountain of debt. We can't keep driving a wider and wider gap between the few who are rich and the rest who struggle to keep pace. It's time to turn the page.

We need a new direction in this country. Everywhere I go, I meet Americans who can't wait another day for change. They're not just showing up to hear a speech—they need to know that politics can make a difference in their lives, that it's not too late to reclaim the American Dream.

It's a dream shared in big cities and small towns; across races, regions, and religions—that if you work hard, you can support a family; that if you get sick, there will be health care you can afford; that you can retire with the dignity and security and respect that you have earned; that your kids can get a good education, and young people can go to college even if they're not rich. That is our common hope. That is the American Dream.

It's the dream of the father who goes to work before dawn and lies awake at night wondering how he's going to pay the bills. He needs us to restore fairness to our economy by putting a tax cut into the pockets of working people, and seniors, and struggling homeowners.

It's the dream of the woman who told me she works the night shift after a full day of college and still can't afford health care for a sister who's ill. She needs us to finally come together to make health care affordable and available for every American.

It's the dream of the senior I met who lost his pension when the company he gave his life to went bankrupt. He doesn't need bankruptcy laws that protect banks and big lenders. He needs us to protect pensions, not CEO bonuses; and to do what it takes to make sure that the American people can count on Social Security today, tomorrow, and forever.

It's the dream of the teacher who works at Dunkin' Donuts after school just to make ends meet. She needs better pay, and more support, and the freedom to do more than just teach to the test. And if her students want to go on to college, they shouldn't fear decades of debt. That's why I'll make college affordable with an annual $4,000 tax credit if you're willing to do community service, or national service. We will invest in you, but we'll ask you to invest in your country.

That is our calling in this campaign. To reaffirm that fundamental belief— I am my brother's keeper, I am my sister's keeper—that makes us one people, and one nation. It's time to stand up and reach for what's possible, because together, people who love their country can change it.

Now when I start talking like this, some folks tell me that I've got my head in the clouds. That I need a reality check. That we're still offering false hope. But my own story tells me that in the United States of America, there has never been anything false about hope.

I should not be here today. I was not born into money or status. I was born to a teenage mom in Hawaii, and my dad left us when I was two. But my family gave me love, they gave me education, and most of all they gave me hope—hope that in America, no dream is beyond our grasp if we reach for it, and fight for it, and work for it.

Because hope is not blind optimism. I know how hard it will be to make these changes. I know this because I fought on the streets of Chicago as a community organizer to bring jobs to the jobless in the shadow of a shuttered steel plant. I've fought in the courts as a civil rights lawyer to make sure people weren't denied their rights because of what they looked like or where they came from.

I've fought in the legislature to take power away from lobbyists. I've won some of those fights, but I've lost some of them too. I've seen good legislation die because good intentions weren't backed by a mandate for change.

> *"Our destiny will not be written for us, but by us."*

The politics of hope does not mean hoping things come easy. Because nothing worthwhile in this country has ever happened unless somebody, somewhere stood up when it was hard; stood up when they were told—no you can't, and said yes we can.

And where better to affirm our ideals than here in Wisconsin, where a century ago the progressive movement was born. It was rooted in the principle that the voices of the people can speak louder than special interests; that citizens can be connected to their government and to one another; and that all of us share a common destiny, an American Dream.

Yes we can reclaim that dream.

Yes we can heal this nation.

The voices of the American people have carried us a great distance on this improbable journey, but we have much further to go. Now we carry our message to farms and factories across this state, and to the cities and small towns of Ohio, to the open plains deep in the heart of Texas, and all the way to the Democratic National Convention in Denver; it's the same message we had when we were up, and when were down; that out of many, we are one; that our destiny will not be written for us, but by us; and that we can cast off our doubts and fears and cynicism because our dream will not be deferred; our future will not be denied; and our time for change has come.

"A More Perfect Union"

Remarks on Race at the National Constitution Center

PHILADELPHIA, PENNSYLVANIA • MARCH 18, 2008

"We the people, in order to form a more perfect union."

Two hundred and twenty one years ago, in a hall that still stands across the street, a group of men gathered and, with these simple words, launched America's improbable experiment in democracy. Farmers and scholars; statesmen and patriots who had traveled across an ocean to escape tyranny and persecution finally made real their declaration of independence at a Philadelphia convention that lasted through the spring of 1787.

The document they produced was eventually signed but ultimately unfinished. It was stained by this nation's original sin of slavery, a question that divided the colonies and brought the convention to a stalemate until the founders chose to allow the slave trade to continue for at least twenty more years, and to leave any final resolution to future generations.

Of course, the answer to the slavery question was already embedded within our Constitution—a Constitution that had at its very core the ideal of equal citizenship under the law; a Constitution that promised its people liberty, and justice, and a union that could be and should be perfected over time.

And yet words on a parchment would not be enough to deliver slaves from bondage, or provide men and women of every color and creed their full rights and obligations as citizens of the United States. What would be needed were Americans in successive generations who were willing to do their part—through protests and struggle, on the streets and in the courts, through a civil war and civil disobedience and always at great risk—to narrow that gap between the promise of our ideals and the reality of their time.

This was one of the tasks we set forth at the beginning of this campaign—to continue the long march of those who came before us, a march for a more just, more equal, more free, more caring, and more prosperous America. I chose to run for the presidency at this moment in history because I believe deeply that we cannot solve the challenges of our time unless we solve them together—unless we perfect our union by understanding that we may have different stories, but we hold common hopes; that we may not look the same and we may not have come from the same place, but we all want to move in the same direction—towards a better future for our children and our grandchildren.

This belief comes from my unyielding faith in the decency and generosity of the American people. But it also comes from my own American story.

I am the son of a black man from Kenya and a white woman from Kansas. I was raised with the help of a white grandfather who survived a Depression to serve in Patton's Army during World War II and a white grandmother who worked on a bomber assembly line at Fort Leavenworth while he was overseas. I've gone to some of the best schools in America and lived in one of the world's poorest nations. I am married to a black American who carries within her the blood of slaves and slaveowners—an inheritance we pass on to our two precious daughters. I have brothers, sisters, nieces, nephews, uncles, and cousins, of every race and every hue, scattered across three continents, and for as long as I live, I will never forget that in no other country on earth is my story even possible.

It's a story that hasn't made me the most conventional candidate. But it is a story that has seared into my genetic makeup the idea that this nation is more than the sum of its parts—that out of many, we are truly one.

Throughout the first year of this campaign, against all predictions to the contrary, we saw how hungry the American people were for this message of

> *"I have asserted a firm conviction—a conviction rooted in my faith in God and my faith in the American people—that working together we can move beyond some of our old racial wounds, and that in fact we have no choice if we are to continue on the path of a more perfect union."*

unity. Despite the temptation to view my candidacy through a purely racial lens, we won commanding victories in states with some of the whitest populations in the country. In South Carolina, where the Confederate flag still flies, we built a powerful coalition of African-Americans and white Americans.

This is not to say that race has not been an issue in the campaign. At various stages in the campaign, some commentators have deemed me either "too black" or "not black enough." We saw racial tensions bubble to the surface during the week before the South Carolina primary. The press has scoured every exit poll for the latest evidence of racial polarization, not just in terms of white and black, but black and brown as well.

And yet, it has only been in the last couple of weeks that the discussion of race in this campaign has taken a particularly divisive turn.

On one end of the spectrum, we've heard the implication that my candidacy is somehow an exercise in affirmative action; that it's based solely on the desire of wide-eyed liberals to purchase racial reconciliation on the cheap. On the other end, we've heard my former pastor, Reverend Jeremiah Wright, use incendiary language to express views that have the potential not only to widen the racial divide, but views that denigrate both the greatness and the goodness of our nation; that rightly offend white and black alike.

I have already condemned, in unequivocal terms, the statements of Reverend Wright that have caused such controversy. For some, nagging questions remain. Did I know him to be an occasionally fierce critic of American domestic and foreign policy? Of course. Did I ever hear him make remarks that could be considered controversial while I sat in church? Yes. Did I strongly disagree with many of his political views? Absolutely—just as I'm sure many of you have heard remarks from your pastors, priests, or rabbis with which you strongly disagreed.

But the remarks that have caused this recent firestorm weren't simply controversial. They weren't simply a religious leader's effort to speak out against perceived injustice. Instead, they expressed a profoundly distorted view of this country—a view that sees white racism as endemic, and that elevates what is wrong with America above all that we know is right with America; a view that sees the conflicts in the Middle East as rooted primarily in the actions of stalwart allies like Israel, instead of emanating from the perverse and hateful ideologies of radical Islam.

As such, Reverend Wright's comments were not only wrong but divisive, divisive at a time when we need unity; racially charged at a time when we need to come together to solve a set of monumental problems—two wars, a terrorist threat, a falling economy, a chronic health care crisis, and potentially devastating climate change; problems that are neither black or white or Latino or Asian, but rather problems that confront us all.

Given my background, my politics, and my professed values and ideals, there will no doubt be those for whom my statements of condemnation are not enough. Why associate myself with Reverend Wright in the first place, they may ask? Why not join another church? And I confess that if all that I knew of Reverend Wright were the snippets of those sermons that have run in an endless loop on the television and You Tube, or if Trinity United Church of Christ conformed to the caricatures being peddled by some commentators, there is no doubt that I would react in much the same way.

But the truth is, that isn't all that I know of the man. The man I met more than twenty years ago is a man who helped introduce me to my Christian faith, a man who spoke to me about our obligations to love one another; to care for the sick and lift up the poor. He is a man who served his country as a U.S. Marine; who has studied and lectured at some of the finest universities and seminaries in the country, and who for over thirty years led a church that serves the community by doing God's work here on earth—by housing the homeless, ministering to the needy, providing day care services and scholarships and prison ministries, and reaching out to those suffering from HIV/AIDS.

In my first book, *Dreams From My Father*, I described the experience of my first service at Trinity:

> People began to shout, to rise from their seats and clap and cry out,
> a forceful wind carrying the reverend's voice up into the rafters…

And in that single note—hope!—I heard something else; at the foot of that cross, inside the thousands of churches across the city, I imagined the stories of ordinary black people merging with the stories of David and Goliath, Moses and Pharaoh, the Christians in the lion's den, Ezekiel's field of dry bones. Those stories—of survival, and freedom, and hope—became our story, my story; the blood that had spilled was our blood, the tears our tears; until this black church, on this bright day, seemed once more a vessel carrying the story of a people into future generations and into a larger world. Our trials and triumphs became at once unique and universal, black and more than black; in chronicling our journey, the stories and songs gave us a means to reclaim memories that we didn't need to feel shame about…memories that all people might study and cherish—and with which we could start to rebuild.

That has been my experience at Trinity. Like other predominantly black churches across the country, Trinity embodies the black community in its entirety—the doctor and the welfare mom, the model student and the former gang-banger. Like other black churches, Trinity's services are full of raucous laughter and sometimes bawdy humor. They are full of dancing, clapping, screaming, and shouting that may seem jarring to the untrained ear. The church contains in full the kindness and cruelty, the fierce intelligence and the shocking ignorance, the struggles and successes, the love and yes, the bitterness and bias that make up the black experience in America.

And this helps explain, perhaps, my relationship with Reverend Wright. As imperfect as he may be, he has been like family to me. He strengthened my faith, officiated my wedding, and baptized my children. Not once in my conversations with him have I heard him talk about any ethnic group in derogatory terms, or treat whites with whom he interacted with anything but courtesy and respect. He contains within him the contradictions—the good and the bad—of the community that he has served diligently for so many years.

I can no more disown him than I can disown the black community. I can no more disown him than I can my white grandmother—a woman who helped raise me, a woman who sacrificed again and again for me, a woman who loves me as much as she loves anything in this world, but a woman who once confessed her fear of black men who passed by her on the street, and who on more than one occasion has uttered racial or ethnic stereotypes that made me cringe.

These people are a part of me. And they are a part of America, this country that I love.

Some will see this as an attempt to justify or excuse comments that are simply inexcusable. I can assure you it is not. I suppose the politically safe thing would be to move on from this episode and just hope that it fades into the woodwork. We can dismiss Reverend Wright as a crank or a demagogue, just as some have dismissed Geraldine Ferraro, in the aftermath of her recent statements, as harboring some deep-seated racial bias.

But race is an issue that I believe this nation cannot afford to ignore right now. We would be making the same mistake that Reverend Wright made in his offending sermons about America—to simplify and stereotype and amplify the negative to the point that it distorts reality.

The fact is that the comments that have been made and the issues that have surfaced over the last few weeks reflect the complexities of race in this country that we've never really worked through—a part of our union that we have yet to perfect. And if we walk away now, if we simply retreat into our respective corners, we will never be able to come together and solve challenges like health care, or education, or the need to find good jobs for every American.

Understanding this reality requires a reminder of how we arrived at this point. As William Faulkner once wrote, "The past isn't dead and buried. In fact, it isn't even past." We do not need to recite here the history of racial injustice in this country. But we do need to remind ourselves that so many of the disparities that exist in the African-American community today can be directly traced to inequalities passed on from an earlier generation that suffered under the brutal legacy of slavery and Jim Crow.

Segregated schools were, and are, inferior schools; we still haven't fixed them, fifty years after Brown v. Board of Education, and the inferior education they provided, then and now, helps explain the pervasive achievement gap between today's black and white students.

Legalized discrimination—where blacks were prevented, often through violence, from owning property, or loans were not granted to African-American business owners, or black homeowners could not access FHA mortgages, or blacks were excluded from unions, or the police force, or fire departments—meant that black families could not amass any meaningful wealth to bequeath to future generations. That history helps explain the wealth and income gap between black and white, and the concentrated pockets of poverty that persists in so many of today's urban and rural communities.

> *"What is remarkable is not how many failed in the face of discrimination, but rather how many men and women overcame the odds; how many were able to make a way out of no way— for those like me who came after them."*

A lack of economic opportunity among black men, and the shame and frustration that came from not being able to provide for one's family, contributed to the erosion of black families—a problem that welfare policies for many years may have worsened. And the lack of basic services in so many urban black neighborhoods—parks for kids to play in, police walking the beat, regular garbage pick-up, and building code enforcement—all helped create a cycle of violence, blight, and neglect that continue to haunt us.

This is the reality in which Reverend Wright and other African-Americans of his generation grew up. They came of age in the late fifties and early sixties, a time when segregation was still the law of the land and opportunity was systematically constricted. What's remarkable is not how many failed in the face of discrimination, but rather how many men and women overcame the odds;

how many were able to make a way out of no way for those like me who would come after them.

But for all those who scratched and clawed their way to get a piece of the American Dream, there were many who didn't make it—those who were ultimately defeated, in one way or another, by discrimination. That legacy of defeat was passed on to future generations—those young men and increasingly young women who we see standing on street corners or languishing in our prisons, without hope or prospects for the future. Even for those blacks who did make it, questions of race, and racism, continue to define their worldview in fundamental ways. For the men and women of Reverend Wright's generation, the memories of humiliation and doubt and fear have not gone away; nor has the anger and the bitterness of those years. That anger may not get expressed in public, in front of white co-workers or white friends. But it does find voice in the barbershop or around the kitchen table. At times, that anger is exploited by politicians, to gin up votes along racial lines, or to make up for a politician's own failings.

And occasionally it finds voice in the church on Sunday morning, in the pulpit and in the pews. The fact that so many people are surprised to hear that anger in some of Reverend Wright's sermons simply reminds us of the old truism that the most segregated hour in American life occurs on Sunday morning. That anger is not always productive; indeed, all too often it distracts attention from solving real problems; it keeps us from squarely facing our own complicity in our condition, and prevents the African-American community from forging the alliances it needs to bring about real change. But the anger is real; it is powerful; and to simply wish it away, to condemn it without understanding its roots, only serves to widen the chasm of misunderstanding that exists between the races.

In fact, a similar anger exists within segments of the white community. Most working- and middle-class white Americans don't feel that they have been particularly privileged by their race. Their experience is the immigrant experience—as far as they're concerned, no one's handed them anything, they've built it from scratch. They've worked hard all their lives, many times only to see their jobs shipped overseas or their pension dumped after a lifetime of labor. They are anxious about their futures, and feel their dreams slipping away; in an era of stagnant wages and global competition, opportunity comes to be seen as a zero sum game, in which your dreams come at my expense. So when they are told to bus their children to a school across town; when they hear that an African-American is getting an advantage in landing a good job or a spot in a good college because of an injustice that they themselves never committed; when they're told that their fears about crime in urban neighborhoods are somehow prejudiced, resentment builds over time.

Like the anger within the black community, these resentments aren't always expressed in polite company. But they have helped shape the political landscape for at least a generation. Anger over welfare and affirmative action helped forge the Reagan Coalition. Politicians routinely exploited fears of crime for their own electoral ends. Talk show hosts and conservative commentators built entire careers unmasking bogus claims of racism while dismissing legitimate discussions of racial injustice and inequality as mere political correctness or reverse racism.

Just as black anger often proved counterproductive, so have these white resentments distracted attention from the real culprits of the middle class squeeze—a corporate culture rife with inside dealing, questionable accounting practices, and short-term greed; a Washington dominated by lobbyists and special interests; economic policies that favor the few over the many. And yet, to wish away the resentments of white Americans, to label them as misguided or even racist, without recognizing they are grounded in legitimate concerns—this too widens the racial divide, and blocks the path to understanding.

This is where we are right now. It's a racial stalemate we've been stuck in for years. Contrary to the claims of some of my critics, black and white, I have never been so naïve as to believe that we can get beyond our racial divisions in a single election cycle, or with a single candidacy—particularly a candidacy as imperfect as my own.

But I have asserted a firm conviction—a conviction rooted in my faith in God and my faith in the American people—that working together we can move beyond some of our old racial wounds, and that in fact we have no choice if we are to continue on the path of a more perfect union.

For the African-American community, that path means embracing the burdens of our past without becoming victims of our past. It means continuing to insist on a full measure of justice in every aspect of American life. But it also means binding our particular grievances—for better health care, and better schools, and better jobs—to the larger aspirations of all Americans—the white woman struggling to break the glass ceiling, the white man whose been laid off, the immigrant trying to feed his family. And it means taking full responsibility for own lives—by demanding more from our fathers, and spending more time with our children, and reading to them, and teaching them that while they may face challenges and discrimination in their own lives, they must never succumb to despair or cynicism; they must always believe that they can write their own destiny.

Ironically, this quintessentially American—and yes, conservative—notion of self-help found frequent expression in Reverend Wright's sermons. But what my former pastor too often failed to understand is that embarking on a program of self-help also requires a belief that society can change.

The profound mistake of Reverend Wright's sermons is not that he spoke about racism in our society. It's that he spoke as if our society was static; as if no progress has been made; as if this country—a country that has made it possible for one of his own members to run for the highest office in the land and build a coalition of white and black, Latino and Asian, rich and poor, young and old—is still irrevocably bound to a tragic past. But what we know—what we have seen—is that America can change. That is the true genius of this nation. What we have already achieved gives us hope—the audacity to hope—for what we can and must achieve tomorrow.

In the white community, the path to a more perfect union means acknowledging that what ails the African-American community does not just exist in the minds of black people; that the legacy of discrimination—and current incidents of discrimination, while less overt than in the past—are real and must be addressed. Not just with words, but with deeds—by investing in our schools and our communities; by enforcing our civil rights laws and ensuring fairness in our criminal justice system; by providing this generation with ladders of opportunity that were unavailable for previous generations. It requires all Americans to realize that your dreams do not have to come at the expense of my dreams; that investing in the health, welfare, and education of black and brown and white children will ultimately help all of America prosper.

In the end, then, what is called for is nothing more, and nothing less, than what all the world's great religions demand—that we do unto others as we would have them do unto us. Let us be our brother's keeper, Scripture tells us. Let us be our sister's keeper. Let us find that common stake we all have in one another, and let our politics reflect that spirit as well.

> " *This union may never be perfect, but generation after generation has shown that it can always be perfected.* "

For we have a choice in this country. We can accept a politics that breeds division, and conflict, and cynicism. We can tackle race only as spectacle— as we did in the OJ trial—or in the wake of tragedy, as we did in the aftermath of Katrina—or as fodder for the nightly news. We can play Reverend Wright's sermons on every channel, every day and talk about them from now until the election, and make the only question in this campaign whether or not the American people think that I somehow believe or sympathize with his most offensive words. We can pounce on some gaffe by a Hillary supporter as evidence that she's playing the race card, or we can speculate on whether white men will all flock to John McCain in the general election regardless of his policies.

We can do that.

But if we do, I can tell you that in the next election, we'll be talking about some other distraction. And then another one. And then another one. And nothing will change.

That is one option. Or, at this moment, in this election, we can come together and say, "Not this time." This time we want to talk about the crumbling schools that are stealing the future of black children and white children and Asian children and Hispanic children and Native American children. This time we want to reject the cynicism that tells us that these kids can't learn; that those kids who don't look like us are somebody else's problem. The children of America are not those kids, they are our kids, and we will not let them fall behind in a 21st-century economy. Not this time.

This time we want to talk about how the lines in the emergency room are filled with whites and blacks and Hispanics who do not have health care; who don't have the power on their own to overcome the special interests in Washington, but who can take them on if we do it together.

This time we want to talk about the shuttered mills that once provided a decent life for men and women of every race, and the homes for sale that once belonged to Americans from every religion, every region, every walk of life. This time we want to talk about the fact that the real problem is not that someone who doesn't look like you might take your job; it's that the corporation you work for will ship it overseas for nothing more than a profit.

This time we want to talk about the men and women of every color and creed who serve together, and fight together, and bleed together under the same proud flag. We want to talk about how to bring them home from a war that never should've been authorized and never should've been waged, and we want to talk about how we'll show our patriotism by caring for them, and their families, and giving them the benefits they have earned.

I would not be running for president if I didn't believe with all my heart that this is what the vast majority of Americans want for this country. This union may never be perfect, but generation after generation has shown that it can always be perfected. And today, whenever I find myself feeling doubtful or cynical about this possibility, what gives me the most hope is the next generation— the young people whose attitudes and beliefs and openness to change have already made history in this election.

There is one story in particular that I'd like to leave you with today—a story I told when I had the great honor of speaking on Dr. King's birthday at his home church, Ebenezer Baptist, in Atlanta.

There is a young, twenty-three-year-old white woman named Ashley Baia who organized for our campaign in Florence, South Carolina. She had been working to organize a mostly African-American community since the beginning of this campaign, and one day she was at a roundtable discussion where everyone went around telling their story and why they were there.

And Ashley said that when she was nine years old, her mother got cancer. And because she had to miss days of work, she was let go and lost her health care. They had to file for bankruptcy, and that's when Ashley decided that she had to do something to help her mom.

She knew that food was one of their most expensive costs, and so Ashley convinced her mother that what she really liked and really wanted to eat more than anything else was mustard and relish sandwiches. Because that was the cheapest way to eat.

She did this for a year until her mom got better, and she told everyone at the roundtable that the reason she joined our campaign was so that she could help the millions of other children in the country who want and need to help their parents too.

Now Ashley might have made a different choice. Perhaps somebody told her along the way that the source of her mother's problems were blacks who were on welfare and too lazy to work, or Hispanics who were coming into the country illegally. But she didn't. She sought out allies in her fight against injustice.

Anyway, Ashley finishes her story and then goes around the room and asks everyone else why they're supporting the campaign. They all have different stories and reasons. Many bring up a specific issue. And finally they come to this elderly black man who's been sitting there quietly the entire time. And Ashley asks him why he's there. And he does not bring up a specific issue. He does not say health care or the economy. He does not say education or the war. He does not say that he was there because of Barack Obama. He simply says to everyone in the room, "I am here because of Ashley."

"I'm here because of Ashley." By itself, that single moment of recognition between that young white girl and that old black man is not enough. It is not enough to give health care to the sick, or jobs to the jobless, or education to our children.

But it is where we start. It is where our union grows stronger. And as so many generations have come to realize over the course of the two-hundred and twenty one years since a band of patriots signed that document in Philadelphia, that is where the perfection begins.

Remembering Dr. Martin Luther King, Jr.

FORT WAYNE, INDIANA • APRIL 4, 2008

As Mike [Rounds] said, today represents a tragic anniversary for our country. Through his faith, courage, and wisdom, Dr. Martin Luther King, Jr. moved an entire nation. He preached the gospel of brotherhood; of equality and justice. That's the cause for which he lived—and for which he died forty years ago today. And so before we begin, I ask you to join me in a moment of silence in memory of this extraordinary American.

There's been a lot of discussion this week about how Dr. King's life and legacy speak to us today. It's taking place in our schools and churches, on television and around the dinner table.

> *"Let's bend that arc toward justice."*

And I suspect that much of what folks are talking about centers on issues of racial justice—on the Montgomery bus boycott and the March on Washington, on the freedom rides and the stand at Selma.

> *"So Dr. King had been to the mountaintop. He had seen the Promised Land. And while he knew somewhere deep in his bones that he would not get there with us, he knew that we would get there."*

And that's as it should be—because those were times when ordinary men and women, straight-backed and clear-eyed, challenged what they knew was wrong and helped perfect our union. And they did so in large part because Dr. King pointed the way.

But I also think it's worth reflecting on what Dr. King was doing in Memphis, when he stepped onto that motel balcony on his way out for dinner.

And what he was doing was standing up for struggling sanitation workers. For years, these workers had served their city without complaint, picking up other people's trash for little pay and even less respect. Passers-by would call them "walking buzzards," and in the segregated South, most were forced to use separate drinking fountains and bathrooms.

But in 1968, these workers decided they'd had enough, and over 1,000 went on strike. Their demands were modest—better wages, better benefits, and recognition of their union. But the opposition was fierce. Their vigils were met with handcuffs. Their protests turned back with mace. And at the end of one march, a sixteen-year-old boy lay dead.

This is the struggle that brought Dr. King to Memphis. It was a struggle for economic justice, for the opportunity that should be available to people of all races and all walks of life. Because Dr. King understood that the struggle for economic justice and the struggle for racial justice were really one—that each was part of a larger struggle "for freedom, for dignity, and for humanity." So long as Americans were trapped in poverty, so long as they were being denied the wages, benefits, and fair treatment they deserved—so long as opportunity was being opened to some but not all—the dream that he spoke of would remain out of reach.

And on the eve of his death, Dr. King gave a sermon in Memphis about what the movement there meant to him and to America. And in tones that would prove eerily prophetic, Dr. King said that despite the threats he'd received, he didn't fear any man, because he had been there when Birmingham aroused the conscience of this nation. And he'd been there to see the students stand up for freedom by sitting in at lunch counters. And he'd been there in Memphis when it was dark enough to see the stars, to see the community coming together around a common purpose. So Dr. King had been to the mountaintop. He had seen the Promised Land. And while he knew somewhere deep in his bones that he would not get there with us, he knew that we would get there.

He knew it because he had seen that Americans have "the capacity," as he said that night, "to project the 'I' into the 'thou.'" To recognize that no matter what the color of our skin, no matter what faith we practice, no matter how much money we have—no matter whether we are sanitation workers or United States Senators—we all have a stake in one another, we are our brother's keeper, we are our sister's keeper, and "either we go up together, or we go down together."

And when he was killed the following day, it left a wound on the soul of our nation that has yet to fully heal. And in few places was the pain more pronounced than in Indianapolis, where Robert Kennedy happened to be campaigning. And it fell to him to inform a crowded park that Dr. King had been killed. And as the shock turned toward anger, Kennedy reminded them of Dr. King's compassion, and his love. And on a night when cities across the nation were alight with violence, all was quiet in Indianapolis.

In the dark days after Dr. King's death, Coretta Scott King pointed out the stars. She took up her husband's cause and led a march in Memphis. But while those sanitation workers eventually got their union contract, the struggle for economic justice remains an unfinished part of the King legacy. Because the dream is still out of reach for too many Americans. Just this morning, it was announced that more Americans are unemployed now than at any time in years. And all across this country, families are facing rising costs, stagnant wages, and the terrible burden of losing a home.

Part of the problem is that for a long time, we've had a politics that's been too small for the scale of the challenges we face. This is something I spoke about a few weeks ago in a speech I gave in Philadelphia. And what I said was that instead of having a politics that lives up to Dr. King's call for unity, we've had a politics that's used race to drive us apart, when all this does is feed the forces of division and distraction, and stop us from solving our problems.

That is why the great need of this hour is much the same as it was when Dr. King delivered his sermon in Memphis. We have to recognize that while we each have a different past, we all share the same hopes for the future—that we'll be able to find a job that pays a decent wage, that there will be affordable health care when we get sick, that we'll be able to send our kids to college, and that after a lifetime of hard work, we'll be able to retire with security. They're common hopes, modest dreams. And they're at the heart of the struggle for freedom, dignity, and humanity that Dr. King began, and that it is our task to complete.

You know, Dr. King once said that the arc of the moral universe is long, but that it bends toward justice. But what he also knew was that it doesn't bend on its own. It bends because each of us puts our hands on that arc and bends it in the direction of justice.

So on this day—of all days—let's each do our part to bend that arc.

Let's bend that arc toward justice.

Let's bend that arc toward opportunity.

Let's bend that arc toward prosperity for all.

And if we can do that and march together—as one nation, and one people—then we won't just be keeping faith with what Dr. King lived and died for, we'll be making real the words of Amos that he invoked so often, and "let justice roll down like water and righteousness like a mighty stream."

A World that Stands as One

Thank you to the citizens of Berlin and to the people of Germany. Let me thank Chancellor Merkel and Foreign Minister Steinmeier for welcoming me earlier today. Thank you Mayor Wowereit, the Berlin Senate, the police, and most of all thank you for this welcome.

I come to Berlin as so many of my countrymen have come before. Tonight, I speak to you not as a candidate for president, but as a citizen—a proud citizen of the United States, and a fellow citizen of the world.

I know that I don't look like the Americans who've previously spoken in this great city. The journey that led me here is improbable. My mother was born in the heartland of America, but my father grew up herding goats in Kenya. His father—my grandfather—was a cook, a domestic servant to the British.

At the height of the Cold War, my father decided, like so many others in the forgotten corners of the world, that his yearning—his dream—required the freedom and opportunity promised by the West. And so he wrote letter after letter to universities all across America until somebody, somewhere answered his prayer for a better life.

That is why I'm here. And you are here because you too know that yearning. This city, of all cities, knows the dream of freedom. And you know that the only reason we stand here tonight is because men and women from both of our nations came together to work, and struggle, and sacrifice for that better life.

Ours is a partnership that truly began sixty years ago this summer, on the day when the first American plane touched down at Templehof.

> " *This city, of all cities, knows the dream of freedom.* "

On that day, much of this continent still lay in ruin. The rubble of this city had yet to be built into a wall. The Soviet shadow had swept across Eastern Europe, while in the West, America, Britain, and France took stock of

> "The walls between old allies on either side of the Atlantic cannot stand. The walls between the countries with the most and those with the least cannot stand. The walls between races and tribes; natives and immigrants; Christian and Muslim and Jew cannot stand. These now are the walls we must tear down."

their losses, and pondered how the world might be remade.

This is where the two sides met. And on the twenty-fourth of June, 1948, the Communists chose to blockade the western part of the city. They cut off food and supplies to more than two million Germans in an effort to extinguish the last flame of freedom in Berlin.

The size of our forces was no match for the much larger Soviet Army. And yet retreat would have allowed Communism to march across Europe. Where the last war had ended, another World War could have easily begun. All that stood in the way was Berlin.

And that's when the airlift began— when the largest and most unlikely rescue in history brought food and hope to the people of this city.

The odds were stacked against success. In the winter, a heavy fog filled the sky above, and many planes were forced to turn back without dropping off the needed supplies. The streets where we stand were filled with hungry families who had no comfort from the cold.

But in the darkest hours, the people of Berlin kept the flame of hope burning. The people of Berlin refused to give up. And on one fall day, hundreds of thousands of Berliners came here, to the Tiergarten, and heard the city's mayor implore the world not to give up on freedom. "There is only one possibility," he said. "For us to stand together united until this battle is won…The people of Berlin have spoken. We have done our duty, and we will keep on doing our duty.

People of the world: now do your duty…People of the world, look at Berlin!"

People of the world—look at Berlin!

Look at Berlin, where Germans and Americans learned to work together and trust each other less than three years after facing each other on the field of battle.

Look at Berlin, where the determination of a people met the generosity of the Marshall Plan and created a German miracle; where a victory over tyranny gave rise to NATO, the greatest alliance ever formed to defend our common security.

Look at Berlin, where the bullet holes in the buildings and the somber stones and pillars near the Brandenburg Gate insist that we never forget our common humanity.

People of the world—look at Berlin, where a wall came down, a continent came together, and history proved that there is no challenge too great for a world that stands as one.

Sixty years after the airlift, we are called upon again. History has led us to a new crossroad, with new promise and new peril. When you, the German people, tore down that wall—a wall that divided East and West; freedom and tyranny; fear and hope—walls came tumbling down around the world. From Kiev to Cape Town, prison camps were closed, and the doors of democracy were opened. Markets opened too, and the spread of information and technology reduced barriers to opportunity and prosperity. While the 20th century taught us that we share a common destiny, the 21st has revealed a world more intertwined than at any time in human history.

The fall of the Berlin Wall brought new hope. But that very closeness has given rise to new dangers—dangers that cannot be contained within the borders of a country or by the distance of an ocean.

The terrorists of September 11th plotted in Hamburg and trained in Kandahar and Karachi before killing thousands from all over the globe on American soil.

As we speak, cars in Boston and factories in Beijing are melting the ice caps in the Arctic, shrinking coastlines in the Atlantic, and bringing drought to farms from Kansas to Kenya.

Poorly secured nuclear material in the former Soviet Union, or secrets from a scientist in Pakistan could help build a bomb that detonates in Paris. The poppies in Afghanistan become the heroin in Berlin. The poverty and violence in Somalia breeds the terror of tomorrow. The genocide in Darfur shames the conscience of us all.

In this new world, such dangerous currents have swept along faster than our efforts to contain them. That is why we cannot afford to be divided. No one nation, no matter how large or powerful, can defeat such challenges alone. None of us can deny these threats, or escape responsibility in meeting them. Yet, in the absence of Soviet tanks and a terrible wall, it has become easy to forget this truth. And if we're honest with each other, we know that sometimes, on both sides of the Atlantic, we have drifted apart, and forgotten our shared destiny.

In Europe, the view that America is part of what has gone wrong in our world, rather than a force to help make it right, has become all too common. In America, there are voices that deride and deny the importance of Europe's role in our security and our future. Both views miss the truth—that Europeans today are bearing new burdens and taking more responsibility in critical parts of the world; and that just as American bases built in the last century still help to defend the security of this continent, so does our country still sacrifice greatly for freedom around the globe.

Yes, there have been differences between America and Europe. No doubt, there will be differences in the future. But the burdens of global citizenship continue to bind us together. A change of leadership in Washington will not lift this burden. In this new century, Americans and Europeans alike will be required to do more—not less. Partnership and cooperation among nations is not a choice; it is the one way, the only way, to protect our common security and advance our common humanity.

That is why the greatest danger of all is to allow new walls to divide us from one another.

The walls between old allies on either side of the Atlantic cannot stand. The walls between the countries with the most and those with the least cannot stand.

The walls between races and tribes; natives and immigrants; Christian and Muslim and Jew cannot stand. These now are the walls we must tear down.

We know they have fallen before. After centuries of strife, the people of Europe have formed a Union of promise and prosperity. Here, at the base of a column built to mark victory in war,

> *"This is the moment when every nation in Europe must have a chance to choose its own tomorrow free from the shadows of yesterday."*

we meet in the center of a Europe at peace. Not only have walls come down in Berlin, but they have come down in Belfast, where Protestant and Catholic found a way to live together; in the Balkans, where our Atlantic alliance ended wars and brought savage war criminals to justice; and in South Africa, where the struggle of a courageous people defeated apartheid.

So history reminds us that walls can be torn down. But the task is never easy. True partnership and true progress requires constant work and sustained sacrifice. They require sharing the burdens of development and diplomacy; of progress and peace. They require allies who will listen to each other, learn from each other and, most of all, trust each other.

That is why America cannot turn inward. That is why Europe cannot turn inward. America has no better partner than Europe. Now is the time to build new bridges across the globe as strong as the one that bound us across the Atlantic. Now is the time to join together, through constant cooperation, strong institutions, shared sacrifice, and a global commitment to progress, to meet the challenges of the 21st century. It was this spirit that led airlift planes to appear in the sky above our heads, and people to assemble where we stand today. And this is the moment when our nations—and all nations—must summon that spirit anew.

This is the moment when we must defeat terror and dry up the well of extremism that supports it. This threat is real and we cannot shrink from our responsibility to combat it. If we could create NATO to face down the Soviet

Union, we can join in a new and global partnership to dismantle the networks that have struck in Madrid and Amman; in London and Bali; in Washington and New York. If we could win a battle of ideas against the communists, we can stand with the vast majority of Muslims who reject the extremism that leads to hate instead of hope.

This is the moment when we must renew our resolve to rout the terrorists who threaten our security in Afghanistan, and the traffickers who sell drugs on your streets. No one welcomes war. I recognize the enormous difficulties in Afghanistan. But my country and yours have a stake in seeing that NATO's first mission beyond Europe's borders is a success. For the people of Afghanistan, and for our shared security, the work must be done. America cannot do this alone. The Afghan people need our troops and your troops; our support and your support to defeat the Taliban and al Qaeda, to develop their economy, and to help them rebuild their nation. We have too much at stake to turn back now.

This is the moment when we must renew the goal of a world without nuclear weapons. The two superpowers that faced each other across the wall of this city came too close too often to destroying all we have built and all that we love. With that wall gone, we need not stand idly by and watch the further spread of the deadly atom. It is time to secure all loose nuclear materials; to stop the spread of nuclear weapons; and to reduce the arsenals from another era. This is the moment to begin the work of seeking the peace of a world without nuclear weapons.

This is the moment when every nation in Europe must have the chance to choose its own tomorrow free from the shadows of yesterday. In this century, we need a strong European Union that deepens the security and prosperity of this continent, while extending a hand abroad. In this century—in this city of all cities—we must reject the Cold War mind-set of the past, and resolve to work with Russia when we can, to stand up for our values when we must, and to seek a partnership that extends across this entire continent.

This is the moment when we must build on the wealth that open markets have created, and share its benefits more equitably. Trade has been a cornerstone of our growth and global development. But we will not be able to sustain this growth if it favors the few, and not the many. Together, we must forge trade that truly rewards the work that creates wealth, with meaningful protections for our people and our planet. This is the moment for trade that is free and fair for all.

This is the moment we must help answer the call for a new dawn in the Middle East. My country must stand with yours and with Europe in sending a direct message to Iran that it must abandon its nuclear ambitions. We must support the Lebanese who have marched and bled for democracy, and the Israelis and Palestinians who seek a secure and lasting peace. And despite past differences, this is the moment when the world should support the millions of Iraqis who seek to rebuild their lives, even as we pass responsibility to the Iraqi government and finally bring this war to a close.

This is the moment when we must come together to save this planet. Let us resolve that we will not leave our children a world where the oceans rise and famine spreads and terrible storms devastate our lands. Let us resolve that all nations—including my own—will act with the same seriousness of purpose as has your nation, and reduce the carbon we send into our atmosphere. This is the moment to give our children back their future. This is the moment to stand as one.

And this is the moment when we must give hope to those left behind in a globalized world. We must remember that the Cold War born in this city was not a battle for land or treasure. Sixty years ago, the planes that flew over Berlin did not drop bombs; instead they delivered food, and coal, and candy to grateful children. And in that show of solidarity, those pilots won more than a military victory. They won hearts and minds; love and loyalty and trust—not just from the people in this city, but from all those who heard the story of what they did here.

Now the world will watch and remember what we do here—what we do with this moment. Will we extend our hand to the people in the forgotten corners of this world who yearn for lives marked by dignity and opportunity; by security and justice? Will we lift the child in Bangladesh from poverty, shelter the refugee in Chad, and banish the scourge of AIDS in our time?

Will we stand for the human rights of the dissident in Burma, the blogger in Iran, or the voter in Zimbabwe? Will we give meaning to the words "never again" in Darfur?

Will we acknowledge that there is no more powerful example than the one each of our nations projects to the world? Will we reject torture and stand for the rule of law? Will we welcome immigrants from different lands, and shun discrimination against those who don't look like us or worship like we do, and keep the promise of equality and opportunity for all of our people?

People of Berlin—people of the world—this is our moment. This is our time.

I know my country has not perfected itself. At times, we've struggled to keep the promise of liberty and equality for all of our people. We've made our share of mistakes, and there are times when our actions around the world have not lived up to our best intentions.

But I also know how much I love America. I know that for more than two centuries, we have strived—at great cost and great sacrifice—to form a more perfect union; to seek, with other nations, a more hopeful world. Our allegiance has never been to any particular tribe or kingdom—indeed, every language is spoken in our country; every culture has left its imprint on ours; every point of view is expressed in our public squares. What has always united us—what has always driven our people; what drew my father to America's shores—is a set of ideals that speak to aspirations shared by all people: that we can live free from fear and free from want; that we can speak our minds and assemble with whomever we choose and worship as we please.

These are the aspirations that joined the fates of all nations in this city. These aspirations are bigger than anything that drives us apart. It is because of these aspirations that the airlift began. It is because of these aspirations that all free people—everywhere—became citizens of Berlin. It is in pursuit of these aspirations that a new generation—our generation—must make our mark on the world.

People of Berlin—and people of the world—the scale of our challenge is great. The road ahead will be long. But I come before you to say that we are heirs to a struggle for freedom. We are a people of improbable hope. With an eye toward the future, with resolve in our hearts, let us remember this history, and answer our destiny, and remake the world once again.

The American Promise

Acceptance Speech, 2008 Democratic National Convention
Denver, Colorado • August 28, 2008

To Chairman Dean and my great friend Dick Durbin; and to all my fellow citizens of this great nation:

With profound gratitude and great humility, I accept your nomination for the presidency of the United States.

Let me express my thanks to the historic slate of candidates who accompanied me on this journey, and especially the one who traveled the farthest—a champion for working Americans and an inspiration to my daughters and to yours—Hillary Rodham Clinton. To President Clinton, who last night made the case for change as only he can make it; to Ted Kennedy, who embodies the spirit of service; and to the next Vice President of the United States, Joe Biden, I thank you. I am grateful to finish this journey with one of the finest statesmen of our time, a man at ease with everyone from world leaders to the conductors on the Amtrak train he still takes home every night.

To the love of my life, our next First Lady, Michelle Obama, and to Sasha and Malia—I love you so much, and I'm so proud of all of you.

Four years ago, I stood before you and told you my story—of the brief union between a young man from Kenya and a young woman from Kansas who weren't well-off or well-known, but shared a belief that in America, their son could achieve whatever he put his mind to.

It is that promise that has always set this country apart—that through hard work and sacrifice, each of us can pursue our individual dreams but still come together as one American family, to ensure that the next generation can pursue their dreams as well.

> " We are more compassionate than a government that lets veterans sleep on our streets and families slide into poverty; that sits on its hands while a major American city drowns before our eyes. "

That's why I stand here tonight. Because for two hundred and thirty two years, at each moment when that promise was in jeopardy, ordinary men and women—students and soldiers, farmers and teachers, nurses and janitors—found the courage to keep it alive.

We meet at one of those defining moments—a moment when our nation is at war, our economy is in turmoil, and the American promise has been threatened once more.

Tonight, more Americans are out of work and more are working harder for less. More of you have lost your homes and even more are watching your home values plummet. More of you have cars you can't afford to drive, credit card bills you can't afford to pay, and tuition that's beyond your reach.

These challenges are not all of government's making. But the failure to respond is a direct result of a broken politics in Washington and the failed policies of George W. Bush.

America, we are better than these last eight years. We are a better country than this.

This country is more decent than one where a woman in Ohio, on the brink of retirement, finds herself one illness away from disaster after a lifetime of hard work.

This country is more generous than one where a man in Indiana has to pack up the equipment he's worked on for twenty years and watch it shipped off to China, and then chokes up as he explains how he felt like a failure when he went home to tell his family the news.

We are more compassionate than a government that lets veterans sleep on our streets and families slide into poverty; that sits on its hands while a major American city drowns before our eyes.

Tonight, I say to the American people, to Democrats and Republicans and Independents across this great land—enough! This moment—this election—is our chance to keep, in the 21st century, the American promise alive. Because next week, in Minnesota, the same party that brought you two terms of George Bush and Dick Cheney will ask this country for a third. And we are here because we love this country too much to let the next four years look like the last eight. On November 4th, we must stand up and say: "Eight is enough."

Now let there be no doubt. The Republican nominee, John McCain, has worn the uniform of our country with bravery and distinction, and for that we owe him our gratitude and respect. And next week, we'll also hear about those occasions when he's broken with his party as evidence that he can deliver the change that we need.

But the record's clear: John McCain has voted with George Bush 90 percent of the time. Senator McCain likes to talk about judgment, but really, what does it say about your judgment when you think George Bush has been right more than 90 percent of the time? I don't know about you, but I'm not ready to take a 10 percent chance on change.

The truth is, on issue after issue that would make a difference in your lives—on health care and education and the economy—Senator McCain has been anything but independent. He said that our economy has made "great progress" under this president. He said that the fundamentals of the economy are strong. And when one of his chief advisors—the man who wrote his economic plan—was talking about the anxiety Americans are feeling, he said that we were just suffering from a "mental recession," and that we've become, and

I quote, "a nation of whiners." A nation of whiners? Tell that to the proud auto workers at a Michigan plant who, after they found out it was closing, kept showing up every day and working as hard as ever, because they knew there were people who counted on the brakes that they made. Tell that to the military families who shoulder their burdens silently as they watch their loved ones leave for their third or fourth or fifth tour of duty. These are not whiners. They work hard and give back and keep going without complaint. These are the Americans that I know.

Now, I don't believe that Senator McCain doesn't care what's going on in the lives of Americans. I just think he doesn't know. Why else would he define middle-class as someone making under five million dollars a year? How else could he propose hundreds of billions in tax breaks for big corporations and oil companies but not one penny of tax relief to more than one hundred million Americans? How else could he offer a health care plan that would actually tax people's benefits, or an education plan that would do nothing to help families pay for college, or a plan that would privatize Social Security and gamble your retirement?

It's not because John McCain doesn't care. It's because John McCain doesn't get it.

For over two decades, he's subscribed to that old, discredited Republican philosophy—give more and more to those with the most and hope that prosperity trickles down to everyone else. In Washington, they call this the Ownership Society, but what it really means is—you're on your own. Out of work? Tough luck. No health care? The market will fix it. Born into poverty? Pull yourself up by your own bootstraps—even if you don't have boots. You're on your own.

Well it's time for them to own their failure. It's time for us to change America.

You see, we Democrats have a very different measure of what constitutes progress in this country.

We measure progress by how many people can find a job that pays the mortgage; whether you can put a little extra money away at the end of each month so you can someday watch your child receive her college diploma. We measure progress in the 23 million new jobs that were created when Bill Clinton was president—when the average American family saw its income go up $7,500 instead of down $2,000 like it has under George Bush.

We measure the strength of our economy not by the number of billionaires we have or the profits of the Fortune 500, but by whether someone with a good idea can take a risk and start a new business, or whether the waitress who lives on tips can take a day off to look after a sick kid without losing her job—an economy that honors the dignity of work.

The fundamentals we use to measure economic strength are whether we are living up to that fundamental promise that has made this country great—a promise that is the only reason I am standing here tonight.

Because in the faces of those young veterans who come back from Iraq and Afghanistan, I see my grandfather, who signed up after Pearl Harbor, marched in Patton's Army, and was rewarded by a grateful nation with the chance to go to college on the GI Bill.

In the face of that young student who sleeps just three hours before working the night shift, I think about my mom, who raised my sister and me on her own while she worked and earned her degree; who once turned to food stamps but was still able to send us to the best schools in the country with the help of student loans and scholarships.

When I listen to another worker tell me that his factory has shut down, I remember all those men and women on the South Side of Chicago who I stood by and fought for two decades ago after the local steel plant closed.

And when I hear a woman talk about the difficulties of starting her own business, I think about my grandmother, who worked her way up from the secretarial pool to middle-management, despite years of being passed over for promotions because she was a woman. She's the one who taught me about hard work. She's the one who put off buying a new car or a new dress for herself so that I could have a better life. She poured everything she had into me. And although she can no longer travel, I know that she's watching

> " We are the party of Roosevelt. We are the party of Kennedy. So don't tell me that Democrats won't defend this country. Don't tell me that Democrats won't keep us safe. "

tonight, and that tonight is her night as well.

I don't know what kind of lives John McCain thinks that celebrities lead, but this has been mine. These are my heroes. Theirs are the stories that shaped me. And it is on their behalf that I intend to win this election and keep our promise alive as President of the United States.

What is that promise?

It's a promise that says each of us has the freedom to make of our own lives what we will, but that we also have the obligation to treat each other with dignity and respect.

It's a promise that says the market should reward drive and innovation and generate growth, but that businesses should live up to their responsibilities to create American jobs, look out for American workers, and play by the rules of the road.

Ours is a promise that says government cannot solve all our problems, but what it should do is that which we cannot do for ourselves—protect us from harm and provide every child a decent education; keep our water clean and our toys safe; invest in new schools and new roads and new science and technology.

Our government should work for us, not against us. It should help us, not hurt us. It should ensure opportunity not just for those with the most money and influence, but for every American who's willing to work.

That's the promise of America—the idea that we are responsible for ourselves, but that we also rise or fall as one nation; the fundamental belief that I am my brother's keeper; I am my sister's keeper.

That's the promise we need to keep. That's the change we need right now. So let me spell out exactly what that change would mean if I am president.

Change means a tax code that doesn't reward the lobbyists who wrote it, but the American workers and small businesses who deserve it.

Unlike John McCain, I will stop giving tax breaks to corporations that ship jobs overseas, and I will start giving them to companies that create good jobs right here in America.

I will eliminate capital gains taxes for the small businesses and the start-ups that will create the high-wage, high-tech jobs of tomorrow.

I will cut taxes—cut taxes—for 95 percent of all working families. Because in an economy like this, the last thing we should do is raise taxes on the middle-class.

And for the sake of our economy, our security, and the future of our planet, I will set a clear goal as president: in ten years, we will finally end our dependence on oil from the Middle East.

Washington's been talking about our oil addiction for the last thirty years, and John McCain has been there for twenty-six of them. In that time, he's said no to higher fuel-efficiency standards for cars, no to investments in renewable energy, no to renewable fuels. And today, we import triple the amount of oil as the day that Senator McCain took office.

Now is the time to end this addiction, and to understand that drilling is a stop-gap measure, not a long-term solution. Not even close.

As president, I will tap our natural gas reserves, invest in clean coal technology, and find ways to safely harness nuclear power. I'll help our auto companies re-tool, so that the fuel-efficient cars of the future are built right here in America. I'll make it easier for the American people to afford these new cars. And I'll invest $150 billion over the next decade in affordable, renewable sources of energy—wind power and solar power and the next generation of biofuels; an investment that will lead to new industries and five million new jobs that pay well and can't ever be outsourced.

America, now is not the time for small plans.

Now is the time to finally meet our moral obligation to provide every child a world-class education, because it will take nothing less to compete in the global economy. Michelle and I are only here tonight because we were given a chance at an education. And I will not settle for an America where some kids don't have that chance. I'll invest in early childhood education. I'll recruit an army of new teachers, and pay them higher salaries and give them more support. And in exchange, I'll ask for higher standards and more accountability. And we will keep our promise to every young American—if you commit to serving your community or your country, we will make sure you can afford a college education.

Now is the time to finally keep the promise of affordable, accessible health care for every single American. If you have health care, my plan will lower your premiums. If you don't, you'll be able to get the same kind of coverage that members of Congress give themselves. And as someone who watched my mother argue with insurance companies while she lay in bed dying of cancer, I will make certain those companies stop discriminating against those who are sick and need care the most.

Now is the time to help families with paid sick days and better family leave, because nobody in America should have to choose between keeping their jobs and caring for a sick child or ailing parent.

Now is the time to change our bankruptcy laws, so that your pensions are protected ahead of CEO bonuses; and the time to protect Social Security for future generations.

And now is the time to keep the promise of equal pay for an equal day's work, because I want my daughters to have exactly the same opportunities as your sons.

Now, many of these plans will cost money, which is why I've laid out how I'll pay for every dime—by closing corporate loopholes and tax havens that don't help America grow. But I will also go through the federal budget, line by line, eliminating programs that no longer work and making the ones we do need work better and cost less—because we cannot meet 21st century challenges with a 20th century bureaucracy.

And Democrats, we must also admit that fulfilling America's promise will require more than just money. It will require a renewed sense of responsibility from each of us to recover what John F. Kennedy called our "intellectual and moral strength." Yes, government must lead on energy independence, but each of us must do our part to make our homes and businesses more efficient. Yes, we must provide more ladders to success for young men who fall into lives of crime and despair. But we must also admit that programs alone can't replace parents; that government can't turn off the television and make a child do her homework; that fathers must take more responsibility for providing the love and guidance their children need.

Individual responsibility and mutual responsibility—that's the essence of America's promise.

And just as we keep our promise to the next generation here at home, so must we keep America's promise abroad. If John McCain wants to have a debate about who has the temperament, and judgment, to serve as the next Commander-in-Chief, that's a debate I'm ready to have.

For while Senator McCain was turning his sights to Iraq just days after 9/11, I stood up and opposed this war, knowing that it would distract us from the real threats we face. When John McCain said we could just "mud-

> *"I will restore our moral standing, so that America is once again that last, best hope for all who are called to the cause of freedom, who long for lives of peace, and who yearn for a better future."*

dle through" in Afghanistan, I argued for more resources and more troops to finish the fight against the terrorists who actually attacked us on 9/11, and made clear that we must take out Osama bin Laden and his lieutenants if we have them in our sights. John McCain likes to say that he'll follow bin Laden to the Gates of Hell—but he won't even go to the cave where he lives.

And today, as my call for a time frame to remove our troops from Iraq has been echoed by the Iraqi government and even the Bush Administration, even after we learned that Iraq has a $79 billion surplus while we're wallowing

> *" It is that American spirit—
> that American promise—
> that pushes us forward even
> when the path is uncertain;
> that binds us together in
> spite of our differences; that
> makes us fix our eye not on
> what is seen, but what is
> unseen, that better place
> around the bend. "*

in deficits, John McCain stands alone in his stubborn refusal to end a misguided war.

That's not the judgment we need. That won't keep America safe. We need a president who can face the threats of the future, not keep grasping at the ideas of the past.

You don't defeat a terrorist network that operates in eighty countries by occupying Iraq. You don't protect Israel and deter Iran just by talking tough in Washington. You can't truly stand up for Georgia when you've strained our oldest alliances. If John McCain wants to follow George Bush with more tough talk and bad strategy, that is his choice—but it is not the change we need.

We are the party of Roosevelt. We are the party of Kennedy. So don't tell me that Democrats won't defend this country. Don't tell me that Democrats won't keep us safe. The Bush-McCain foreign policy has squandered the legacy that generations of Americans—Democrats and Republicans—have built, and we are here to restore that legacy.

As Commander-in-Chief, I will never hesitate to defend this nation, but I will only send our troops into harm's way with a clear mission and a sacred commitment to give them the equipment they need in battle and the care and benefits they deserve when they come home.

I will end this war in Iraq responsibly, and finish the fight against al Qaeda and the Taliban in Afghanistan. I will rebuild our military to meet future conflicts. But I will also renew the tough, direct diplomacy that can prevent Iran from obtaining nuclear weapons and curb Russian aggression. I will build new partnerships to defeat the threats of the 21st century: terrorism and nuclear proliferation; poverty and genocide; climate change and disease. And I will restore our moral standing, so that America is once again that last, best hope for all who are called to the cause of freedom, who long for lives of peace, and who yearn for a better future.

These are the policies I will pursue. And in the weeks ahead, I look forward to debating them with John McCain.

But what I will not do is suggest that the Senator takes his positions for political purposes. Because one of the things that we have to change in our politics is the idea that people cannot disagree without challenging each other's character and patriotism.

The times are too serious, the stakes are too high for this same partisan playbook. So let us agree that patriotism has no party. I love this country, and so do you, and so does John McCain. The men and women who serve in our battlefields may be Democrats and Republicans and Independents, but they have fought together and bled together and some died together under the same proud flag. They have not served a Red America or a Blue America—they have served the United States of America.

So I've got news for you, John McCain. We all put our country first.

America, our work will not be easy. The challenges we face require tough choices, and Democrats as well as Republicans will need to cast off the worn-out ideas and politics of the past. For part of what has been lost these past eight years can't just be measured by lost wages or bigger trade deficits. What has also been lost is our sense of common purpose—our sense of higher purpose. And that's what we have to restore.

We may not agree on abortion, but surely we can agree on reducing the number of unwanted pregnancies in this country. The reality of gun ownership may be different for hunters in rural Ohio than for those plagued by gang-violence in Cleveland, but don't tell me we can't uphold the Second Amendment while keeping AK-47s out of the hands of criminals. I know there are differences on same-sex marriage, but surely we can agree that our gay and lesbian brothers and sisters deserve to visit the person they love in the hospital and to live lives free of discrimination. Passions fly on immigration, but I don't know anyone who benefits when a mother is separated from her infant child or an employer undercuts American wages by hiring illegal workers. This too is part of America's promise—the promise of a democracy where we can find the strength and grace to bridge divides and unite in common effort.

I know there are those who dismiss such beliefs as happy talk. They claim that our insistence on something larger, something firmer and more honest in our public life is just a Trojan horse for higher taxes and the abandonment of traditional values. And that's to be expected. Because if you don't have any fresh ideas, then you use stale tactics to scare the voters. If you don't have a record to run on, then you paint your opponent as someone people should run from.

You make a big election about small things.

And you know what—it's worked before. Because it feeds into the cynicism we all have about government. When Washington doesn't work, all its promises seem empty. If your hopes have been dashed again and again, then it's best to stop hoping, and settle for what you already know.

I get it. I realize that I am not the likeliest candidate for this office. I don't fit the typical pedigree, and I haven't spent my career in the halls of Washington.

But I stand before you tonight because all across America something is stirring. What the naysayers don't understand is that this election has never been about me. It's been about you.

For eighteen long months, you have stood up, one by one, and said enough to the politics of the past. You understand that in this election, the greatest risk we can take is to try the same old politics with the same old players and expect a different result. You have shown what history teaches us—that at defining moments like this one, the change we need doesn't come from Washington. Change comes to Washington. Change happens because the American people demand it—because they rise up and insist on new ideas and new leadership, a new politics for a new time.

America, this is one of those moments.

I believe that as hard as it will be, the change we need is coming. Because I've seen it. Because I've lived it. I've seen it in Illinois, when we provided health care to more children and moved more families from welfare to work. I've seen it in Washington, when we worked across party lines to open up government and hold lobbyists more accountable, to give better care for our veterans and keep nuclear weapons out of terrorist hands.

> *"America, we cannot turn back."*

And I've seen it in this campaign. In the young people who voted for the first time, and in those who got involved again after a very long time. In the Republicans who never thought they'd pick up a Democratic ballot, but did. I've seen it in the workers who would rather cut their hours back a day than see their friends lose their jobs, in the soldiers who re-enlist after losing a limb, in the good neighbors who take a stranger in when a hurricane strikes and the floodwaters rise.

This country of ours has more wealth than any nation, but that's not what makes us rich. We have the most powerful military on earth, but that's not what makes us strong. Our universities and our culture are the envy of the world, but that's not what keeps the world coming to our shores.

Instead, it is that American spirit—that American promise—that pushes us forward even when the path is uncertain; that binds us together in spite of our differences; that makes us fix our eye not on what is seen, but what is unseen, that better place around the bend.

That promise is our greatest inheritance. It's a promise I make to my daughters when I tuck them in at night, and a promise that you make to yours—a promise that has led immigrants to cross oceans and pioneers to travel west; a promise that led workers to picket lines, and women to reach for the ballot.

And it is that promise that forty five years ago today, brought Americans from every corner of this land to stand together on a Mall in Washington, before Lincoln's Memorial, and hear a young preacher from Georgia speak of his dream.

The men and women who gathered there could've heard many things. They could've heard words of anger and discord. They could've been told to succumb to the fear and frustration of so many dreams deferred.

But what the people heard instead—people of every creed and color, from every walk of life—is that in America, our destiny is inextricably linked. That together, our dreams can be one.

"We cannot walk alone," the preacher cried. "And as we walk, we must make the pledge that we shall always march ahead. We cannot turn back."

America, we cannot turn back. Not with so much work to be done. Not with so many children to educate, and so many veterans to care for. Not with an economy to fix and cities to rebuild and farms to save. Not with so many families to protect and so many lives to mend. America, we cannot turn back. We cannot walk alone. At this moment, in this election, we must pledge once more to march into the future. Let us keep that promise—that American promise—and in the words of Scripture hold firmly, without wavering, to the hope that we confess.

Thank you, God Bless you, and God Bless the United States of America.

The Change We Need

General Election Campaign Speech

PHILADELPHIA, PENNSYLVANIA • OCTOBER 11, 2008

We meet at a moment of great uncertainty for America. In recent weeks, we've seen a growing financial crisis that's threatening not only banks and businesses, but your economic security as well. It's getting harder to get a loan for that new car or that small business or that college you've dreamed of attending. And in recent days, millions of Americans have lost more of their investments and hard-earned retirement savings as the stock market has plunged.

I know these are difficult times. I know folks are worried. But I also know that now is not the time for fear or panic. Now is the time for resolve and steady leadership. Because I know we can steer ourselves out of this crisis. This is a nation that has faced down war and depression; great challenges and

> "*We have always risen to the moment when the moment was hard—and we can do it again.*"

great threats. We have always seen that mountaintop from the deepest valley. We have always risen to the moment when the moment was hard—and we can do it again. We can restore confidence in our economy and renew that fundamental belief—that here in America, our destiny is not written for us, but by us.

America is home to colleges and universities that are the envy of the world, and some of the biggest ideas and innovations in history have come from our small businesses. We've got the hardest workers on earth—folks who work two jobs or three jobs and take that last bus home at night because they want something more for their children. And no one works harder than folks here in Pennsylvania—just ask my friend, Joe Biden, he'll tell you. So while it won't be easy, there is no reason we can't make this century another American century.

Unfortunately, my opponent still sees things differently. Now, I want to acknowledge that Senator McCain tried to tone down the rhetoric yesterday, and I appreciated his reminder that we can disagree while still being respectful of each other. I've said it before, and I'll say it again—Senator McCain has served this country with honor, and he deserves our thanks for that.

But when it comes to the economy, and what families here in Pennsylvania are going through, Senator McCain still doesn't get it. Yesterday, Senator McCain's campaign manager actually said that Senator McCain wasn't talking about the market because there's just not much a candidate for president can say—and they aren't sure what he'd say each day even if he did talk about it. Last week, in the midst of the most serious economic crisis of our time, his campaign announced that they plan to "turn the page" on the discussion about our economy so they can spend the final weeks of this election attacking me instead. They said, and I quote, "If we keep talking about the economy, we're going to lose." So the last few days, we've seen a barrage of nasty insinuations and attacks, and I'm sure we'll see much more over the next twenty-four days.

But here's the thing. They can run misleading ads, and pursue the politics of anything goes, and try to change the subject. They can do that—but it's not going to work. Not this time.

> " *This country and the dream it represents are being tested in a way that we haven't seen in nearly a century.* "

The times are too serious. The challenges are too great. The American people aren't looking for someone who can divide this country—they're looking for someone who will lead it.

We simply cannot afford four more years of the economic theory that says we should give more to those with the most and hope prosperity trickles down to everyone else.

It is time to turn the page on eight years of economic policies that put Wall Street before Main Street but end up hurting both. We need policies that grow our economy from the bottom-up, so that every American, everywhere has the chance to get ahead. Not just corporate CEOs, but their secretaries too. Not just the person who owns the factory, but the men and women who work on its floor.

These are the Americans I'm standing with. These are the folks I'm fighting for. That's the kind of leadership I'm offering. That's what I mean when I talk about change.

Change means rebuilding this economy. We know that it's time to create the good-paying jobs of tomorrow. Pennsylvania is hurting. Thousands of jobs have been lost this year and wages are flat-lining. But it doesn't have to be this way. That's why I'm going to stop giving tax breaks to companies that ship jobs overseas, and start rebuilding the middle class by helping companies create jobs here in Pennsylvania. I will be a president who puts you first, Pennsylvania. Because I believe in the American people and what we can do together. And if we want to turn this economy around and lead the world in the 21st century, we have to create the high-wage jobs of tomorrow right here in America.

So we'll invest $15 billion a year in renewable energy to create five million new, green jobs over the next decade—jobs that pay well and can't be outsourced. And we'll provide affordable loans for our small businesses, eliminate their capital gains taxes, and give them tax incentives to create new jobs. That's the change we need.

Change means a tax code that doesn't just work for folks at the top—but for all of us. While my opponent wants to give $200 billion in tax cuts to the biggest corporations in America, and $700,000 a piece for the average Fortune 500 CEO—I'll give a middle-class tax cut to 95 percent of all workers. And if you make less than $250,000 a year, you won't see your taxes increase one single dime—not your payroll taxes, not your income taxes, not your capital gains taxes—nothing. Because in an economy like this, the last thing we should do is raise taxes on the middle class.

Change means finally fixing our health care system. Under my plan, if you have health insurance, the only thing that will change is that you'll pay lower premiums. If you don't have insurance, you'll be able to get the same kind of health insurance that members of Congress get for themselves. We'll give small businesses a tax credit to pay 50 percent of the cost of covering their employees. And we'll tell insurance companies, no more discriminating against people with pre-existing conditions, period. That's the change we need.

Change means giving every child, everywhere the skills and knowledge they need to compete with any worker, anywhere in the world. That means investing in early childhood education, and recruiting an army of new teachers, and making a deal with every American who has the drive and the will but not the money to go to college: if you commit to serving your country after you graduate, we will make sure you can afford your tuition. You invest in America, America will invest in you, and together, we will move this country forward.

Finally, change means taking on the corruption in Washington and on Wall Street to make sure a crisis like this can never happen again. I'll put in place commonsense regulations to keep our market free and fair and restore accountability and responsibility in our boardrooms.

And I'll go through the entire federal budget, line by line, and eliminate any spending that isn't helping our families. And you know where I'll start? By ending this war in Iraq that's costing $10 billion a month while the Iraqi government sits on tens of billions of dollars in surplus.

I won't pretend this will be easy or come without cost. We will all need to sacrifice, and we will all need to pull our weight, because now more than ever, we are all in this together. This country and the dream it represents are being tested in a way that we haven't seen in nearly a century.

It's a test we cannot fail. Not now. Not when we have a crisis to solve and an economy to save. Not when there are so many Americans without jobs and without homes. Not when there are families who can't afford to see a doctor, or send their child to college. Not when there is a generation that is counting on us to give them the same opportunities and the same chances that we had for ourselves.

We can do this. We've done it before. Some of us had grandparents or parents who said maybe I can't go to college but my child can; maybe I can't have my own business but my child can. I may have to rent, but maybe my children will have a home they can call their own. I may not have a lot of money, but maybe my child will run for Senate. I might live in a small village, but maybe someday my son can be president of the United States of America.

And if you keep standing with me, if you keep fighting with me, if you keep making those calls, and knocking on those doors, and making sure everyone you know gets out to the polls on November 4th—if you do these things, then I promise you, we will win this election, and then you and I—together—will change this country and change this world. Thank you, God bless you, and may God bless America.

Change Has Come to America

Election Night Victory Speech in Grant Park

CHICAGO, ILLINOIS • NOVEMBER 4, 2008

If there is anyone out there who still doubts that America is a place where all things are possible; who still wonders if the dream of our founders is alive in our time; who still questions the power of our democracy, tonight is your answer.

It's the answer told by lines that stretched around schools and churches in numbers this nation has never seen; by people who waited three hours and four hours, many for the very first time in their lives, because they believed that this time must be different; that their voice could be that difference.

It's the answer spoken by young and old, rich and poor, Democrat and Republican, black, white, Latino, Asian, Native American, gay, straight, disabled and not disabled—Americans who sent a message to the world that we have never been a collection of Red States and Blue States: we are, and always will be, the United States of America.

It's the answer that led those who have been told for so long by so many to be cynical, and fearful, and doubtful of what we can achieve to put their hands on the arc of history and bend it once more toward the hope of a better day.

"What began twenty-one months ago in the depths of winter must not end on this autumn night."

It's been a long time coming, but tonight, because of what we did on this day, in this election, at this defining moment, change has come to America.

I just received a very gracious call from Senator McCain. He fought long and hard in this campaign, and he's fought even longer and harder for the country he loves. He has endured sacrifices for America that most of us cannot begin to imagine, and we are better off for the service rendered by this brave and selfless leader. I congratulate him and

Governor Palin for all they have achieved, and I look forward to working with them to renew this nation's promise in the months ahead.

I want to thank my partner in this journey, a man who campaigned from his heart and spoke for the men and women he grew up with on the streets of Scranton and rode with on that train home to Delaware, the Vice President-elect of the United States, Joe Biden.

> *"It's the answer that led those who have been told for so long by so many to be cynical, and fearful, and doubtful of what we can achieve to put their hands on the arc of history and bend it once more toward the hope of a better day."*

I would not be standing here tonight without the unyielding support of my best friend for the last sixteen years, the rock of our family and the love of my life, our nation's next First Lady, Michelle Obama. Sasha and Malia, I love you both more than you can imagine, and you have earned the new puppy that's coming with us to the White House. And while she's no longer with us, I know my grandmother is watching, along with the family that made me who I am. I miss them tonight, and know that my debt to them is beyond measure.

To my campaign manager David Plouffe, my chief strategist David Axelrod, and the best campaign team ever assembled in the history of politics—you made this happen, and I am forever grateful for what you've sacrificed to get it done.

But above all, I will never forget who this victory truly belongs to—it belongs to you.

I was never the likeliest candidate for this office. We didn't start with much money or many endorsements. Our campaign was not hatched in the halls of Washington—it began in the backyards of Des Moines and the living rooms of Concord and the front porches of Charleston.

It was built by working men and women who dug into what little savings they had to give five dollars and ten dollars and twenty dollars to this cause. It grew strength from the young people who rejected the myth of their generation's apathy; who left their homes and their families for jobs that offered little pay and less sleep; from the not-so-young people who braved the bitter cold and scorching heat to knock on the doors of perfect strangers; from the millions of Americans who volunteered, and organized, and proved that more than two centuries later, a government of the people, by the people and for the people has not perished from this Earth. This is your victory.

I know you didn't do this just to win an election and I know you didn't do it for me. You did it because you understand the enormity of the task that lies ahead. For even as we celebrate tonight, we know the challenges that tomorrow will bring are the greatest of our lifetime—two wars, a planet in peril, the worst financial crisis in a century. Even as we stand here tonight, we know there are brave Americans waking up in the deserts of Iraq and the mountains of Afghanistan to risk their lives for us. There are mothers and fathers who will lie awake after their children fall asleep and wonder how they'll make the mortgage, or pay their doctor's bills, or save enough for college. There is new energy to harness and new jobs to be created; new schools to build and threats to meet and alliances to repair.

The road ahead will be long. Our climb will be steep. We may not get there in one year or even one term, but America—I have never been more hopeful than I am tonight that we will get there. I promise you—we as a people will get there.

There will be setbacks and false starts. There are many who won't agree with every decision or policy I make as president, and we know that government can't solve every problem. But I will always be honest with you about the challenges we face. I will listen to you, especially when we disagree. And above all, I will ask you join in the work of remaking this nation the only way it's

> *"And to those Americans whose support I have yet to earn—I may not have won your vote, but I hear your voices, I need your help, and I will be your president too."*

been done in America for two-hundred and twenty-one years—block by block, brick by brick, calloused hand by calloused hand.

> " Tonight we proved once more that the true strength of our nation comes not from the might of our arms or the scale of our wealth, but from the enduring power of our ideals: democracy, liberty, opportunity, and unyielding hope. "

What began twenty-one months ago in the depths of winter must not end on this autumn night. This victory alone is not the change we seek—it is only the chance for us to make that change. And that cannot happen if we go back to the way things were. It cannot happen without you.

So let us summon a new spirit of patriotism; of service and responsibility where each of us resolves to pitch in and work harder and look after not only ourselves, but each other. Let us remember that if this financial crisis taught us anything, it's that we cannot have a thriving Wall Street while Main Street suffers—in this country, we rise or fall as one nation; as one people.

Let us resist the temptation to fall back on the same partisanship and pettiness and immaturity that has poisoned our politics for so long. Let us remember that it was a man from this state who first carried the banner of the Republican Party to the White House—a party founded on the values of self-reliance, individual liberty, and national unity. Those are values we all share, and while the Democratic Party has won a great victory tonight, we do so with a measure of humility and determination to heal the divides that have held back our progress. As Lincoln said to a nation far more divided than ours, "We are not enemies, but friends…though passion may have strained it must not break our bonds of affection." And to those Americans whose support I have yet to earn—I may not have won your vote, but I hear your voices, I need your help, and I will be your president too.

And to all those watching tonight from beyond our shores, from parliaments and palaces to those who are huddled around radios in the forgotten corners of our world—our stories are singular, but our destiny is shared, and a new dawn of American leadership is at hand. To those who would tear this world down—we will defeat you. To those who seek peace and security—we support you. And to all those who have wondered if America's beacon still burns as bright—tonight we proved once more that the true strength of our nation comes not from our the might of our arms or the scale of our wealth, but from the enduring power of our ideals: democracy, liberty, opportunity, and unyielding hope.

For that is the true genius of America—that America can change. Our union can be perfected. And what we have already achieved gives us hope for what we can and must achieve tomorrow.

This election had many firsts and many stories that will be told for generations. But one that's on my mind tonight is about a woman who cast her ballot in Atlanta. She's a lot like the millions of others who stood in line to make their voice heard in this election except for one thing—Ann Nixon Cooper is 106 years old.

She was born just a generation past slavery; a time when there were no cars on the road or planes in the sky; when someone like her couldn't vote for two reasons—because she was a woman and because of the color of her skin.

And tonight, I think about all that she's seen throughout her century in America—the heartache and the hope; the struggle and the progress; the times we were told that we can't, and the people who pressed on with that American creed: Yes we can.

At a time when women's voices were silenced and their hopes dismissed, she lived to see them stand up and speak out and reach for the ballot. Yes we can.

When there was despair in the dust bowl and depression across the land, she saw a nation conquer fear itself with a New Deal, new jobs, and a new sense of common purpose. Yes we can.

> *"That timeless creed that sums up the spirit of a people: Yes we can."*

When the bombs fell on our harbor and tyranny threatened the world, she was there to witness a generation rise to greatness and a democracy was saved. Yes we can.

She was there for the buses in Montgomery, the hoses in Birmingham, a bridge in Selma, and a preacher from Atlanta who told a people that "We Shall Overcome." Yes we can.

A man touched down on the moon, a wall came down in Berlin, a world was connected by our own science and imagination. And this year, in this election, she touched her finger to a screen, and cast her vote, because after 106 years in America, through the best of times and the darkest of hours, she knows how America can change. Yes we can.

America, we have come so far. We have seen so much. But there is so much more to do. So tonight, let us ask ourselves—if our children should live to see the next century, if my daughters should be so lucky to live as long as Ann Nixon Cooper—what change will they see? What progress will we have made?

This is our chance to answer that call. This is our moment. This is our time—to put our people back to work and open doors of opportunity for our kids; to restore prosperity and promote the cause of peace; to reclaim the American Dream and reaffirm that fundamental truth—that out of many, we are one; that while we breathe, we hope; and where we are met with cynicism, and doubt, and those who tell us that we can't, we will respond with that timeless creed that sums up the spirit of a people: Yes we can. Thank you, God Bless you, and may God Bless the United States of America.

American Recovery and Reinvestment

FAIRFAX, VIRGINIA • JANUARY 8, 2009

Throughout America's history, there have been some years that simply rolled into the next without much notice or fanfare. Then there are the years that come along once in a generation—the kind that mark a clean break from a troubled past, and set a new course for our nation.

This is one of those years.

We start 2009 in the midst of a crisis unlike any we have seen in our lifetime—a crisis that has only deepened over the last few weeks. Nearly two million jobs have now been lost, and on Friday we are likely to learn that we lost more jobs last year than at any time since World War II. Just in the past year, another 2.8 million Americans who want and need full-time work have had to settle for part-time jobs. Manufacturing has hit a twenty-eight year low. Many businesses cannot borrow or make payroll. Many families cannot pay their bills or their mortgage. Many workers are watching their life savings disappear. And many, many Americans are both anxious and uncertain of what the future will hold.

I don't believe it's too late to change course, but it will be if we don't take dramatic action as soon as possible. If nothing is done, this recession could linger for years. The unemployment rate could reach double digits. Our economy could fall $1 trillion short of its full capacity, which translates into more than $12,000 in lost income for a family of four. We could lose a generation of potential and promise, as more young Americans are forced to forgo dreams of college or the chance to train for the jobs of the future. And our nation could lose the competitive edge that has served as a foundation for our strength and standing in the world.

In short, a bad situation could become dramatically worse.

This crisis did not happen solely by some accident of history or normal turn of the business cycle, and we won't get out of it by simply waiting for a better day to come, or relying on the worn-out dogmas of the past. We arrived at this point due to an era of profound irresponsibility that stretched from corporate board-

> "We are still home to the most brilliant minds, the most creative entrepreneurs, and the most advanced technology and innovation that history has ever known."

rooms to the halls of power in Washington, D.C. For years, too many Wall Street executives made imprudent and dangerous decisions, seeking profits with too little regard for risk, too little regulatory scrutiny, and too little accountability. Banks made loans without concern for whether borrowers could repay them, and some borrowers took advantage of cheap credit to take on debt they couldn't afford. Politicians spent taxpayer money without wisdom or discipline, and too often focused on scoring political points instead of the problems they were sent here to solve. The result has been a devastating loss of trust and confidence in our economy, our financial markets, and our government.

Now, the very fact that this crisis is largely of our own making means that it is not beyond our ability to solve. Our problems are rooted in past mistakes, not our capacity for future greatness. It will take time, perhaps many years, but we can rebuild that lost trust and confidence. We can restore opportunity and prosperity. We should never forget that our workers are still more productive than any on earth. Our universities are still the envy of the world. We are still home to the most brilliant minds, the most creative entrepreneurs, and the most advanced technology and innovation that history has ever known. And we are still the nation that has overcome great fears and improbable odds. If we act with the urgency and seriousness that this moment requires, I know that we can do it again.

That is why I have moved quickly to work with my economic team and leaders of both parties on an American Recovery and Reinvestment Plan that will immediately jump-start job creation and long-term growth.

It's a plan that represents not just new policy, but a whole new approach to meeting our most urgent challenges. For if we hope to end this crisis, we must end the culture of anything goes that helped create it—and this change must begin in Washington. It is time to trade old habits for a new spirit of responsibility. It is time to finally change the ways of Washington so that we can set a new and better course for America.

There is no doubt that the cost of this plan will be considerable. It will certainly add to the budget deficit in the short term. But equally certain are the consequences of doing too little or nothing at all, for that will lead to an even greater deficit of jobs, incomes, and confidence in our economy. It is true that we cannot depend on government alone to create jobs or long-term growth, but at this particular moment, only government can provide the short-term boost necessary to lift us from a recession this deep and severe. Only government can break the vicious cycles that are crippling our economy—where a lack of spending leads to lost jobs which leads to even less spending; where an inability to lend and borrow stops growth and leads to even less credit.

That is why we need to act boldly and act now to reverse these cycles. That's why we need to put money in the pockets of the American people, create new jobs, and invest in our future. That's why we need to restart the flow of credit and restore the rules of the road that will ensure a crisis like this never happens again.

That work begins with this plan—a plan I am confident will save or create at least three million jobs over the next few years. It is not just another public works program. It's a plan that recognizes both the paradox and the promise of this moment—the fact that there are millions of Americans trying to find work, even as, all around the country, there is so much work to be done. That's why we'll invest in priorities like energy and education, health care and a new infrastructure that are necessary to keep us strong and competitive in the 21st century. That's why the overwhelming majority of the jobs created will be in the private sector, while our plan will save the public sector jobs of teachers, cops, firefighters, and others who provide vital services.

To finally spark the creation of a clean energy economy, we will double the production of alternative energy in the next three years. We will modernize

> *"A world that depends on the strength of our economy is now watching and waiting for America to lead once more. And that is what we will do."*

more than 75 percent of federal buildings and improve the energy efficiency of two million American homes, saving consumers and taxpayers billions on our energy bills. In the process, we will put Americans to work in new jobs that pay well and can't be outsourced— jobs building solar panels and wind turbines; constructing fuel-efficient cars and buildings; and developing the new energy technologies that will lead to even more jobs, more savings, and a cleaner, safer planet in the bargain.

To improve the quality of our health care while lowering its cost, we will make the immediate investments necessary to ensure that within five years, all of America's medical records are computerized. This will cut waste, eliminate red tape, and reduce the need to repeat expensive medical tests. But it just won't [*sic*] save billions of dollars and thousands of jobs—it will save lives by reducing the deadly but preventable medical errors that pervade our health care system.

To give our children the chance to live out their dreams in a world that's never been more competitive, we will equip tens of thousands of schools, community colleges, and public universities with 21st century classrooms, labs, and libraries. We'll provide new computers, new technology, and new training for teachers so that students in Chicago and Boston can compete with kids in Beijing for the high-tech, high-wage jobs of the future.

To build an economy that can lead this future, we will begin to rebuild America. Yes, we'll put people to work repairing crumbling roads, bridges, and schools by eliminating the backlog of well-planned, worthy and needed infrastructure projects. But we'll also do more to retrofit America for a global economy. That means updating the way we get our electricity by starting to build a new smart grid that will save us money, protect our power sources from blackout or attack, and deliver clean, alternative forms of energy to every corner of our nation. It means expanding broadband lines across America, so that a small business in a rural town can connect and compete with their counterparts anywhere in the world. And it means investing in the science, research, and technology that will lead to new medical breakthroughs, new discoveries, and entire new industries.

Finally, this recovery and reinvestment plan will provide immediate relief to states, workers, and families who are bearing the brunt of this recession. To get people spending again, 95 percent of working families will receive a $1,000 tax cut—the first stage of a middle-class tax cut that I promised during the campaign and will include in our next budget. To help Americans who have lost their jobs and can't find new ones, we'll continue the bipartisan extensions of unemployment insurance and health care coverage to help them through this crisis. Government at every level will have to tighten its belt, but we'll help struggling states avoid harmful budget cuts, as long as they take responsibility and use the money to maintain essential services like police, fire, education, and health care.

I understand that some might be skeptical of this plan. Our government has already spent a good deal of money, but we haven't yet seen that translate into more jobs or higher incomes or renewed confidence in our economy. That's why the American Recovery and Reinvestment Plan won't just throw money at our problems—we'll invest in what works. The true test of the policies we'll pursue won't be whether they're Democratic or Republican ideas, but whether they create jobs, grow our economy, and put the American Dream within reach of the American people.

Instead of politicians doling out money behind a veil of secrecy, decisions about where we invest will be made transparently, and informed by independent experts wherever possible. Every American will be able to hold Washington accountable for these decisions by going online to see how and where their tax dollars are being spent. And as I announced yesterday, we will launch an unprecedented effort to eliminate unwise and unnecessary spending that has never been more unaffordable for our nation and our children's future than it is right now.

> *"That's why I'm calling on all Americans—Democrats and Republicans—to insist that the first question each of us asks isn't 'What's good for me?' but 'What's good for the country my children will inherit?'"*

We have to make tough choices and smart investments today so that as the economy recovers, the deficit starts to come down. We cannot have a solid recovery if our people and our businesses don't have confidence that we're getting our fiscal house in order. That's why our goal is not to create a slew of new government programs, but a foundation for long-term economic growth.

That also means an economic recovery plan that is free from earmarks and pet projects. I understand that every member of Congress has ideas on how to spend money. Many of these projects are worthy, and benefit local communities. But this emergency legislation must not be the vehicle for those aspirations. This must be a time when leaders in both parties put the urgent needs of our nation above our own narrow interests.

Now, this recovery plan alone will not solve all the problems that led us into this crisis. We must also work with the same sense of urgency to stabilize and repair the financial system we all depend on. That means using our full arsenal of tools to get credit flowing again to families and business, while restoring confidence in our markets. It means launching a sweeping effort to address the foreclosure crisis so that we can keep responsible families in their homes. It means preventing the catastrophic failure of financial institutions whose collapse could endanger the entire economy, but only with maximum protections for taxpayers and a clear understanding that government support for any company is an extraordinary action that must come with significant restrictions on the firms that receive support. And it means reforming a weak and outdated regulatory system so that we can better withstand financial shocks and better protect consumers, investors, and businesses from the reckless greed and risk-taking that must never endanger our prosperity again.

No longer can we allow Wall Street wrongdoers to slip through regulatory cracks. No longer can we allow special interests to put their thumbs on the economic scales. No longer can we allow the unscrupulous lending and borrowing that leads only to destructive cycles of bubble and bust.

It is time to set a new course for this economy, and that change must begin now. We should have an open and honest discussion about this recovery plan in the days ahead, but I urge Congress to move as quickly as possible on behalf of the American people. For every day we wait or point fingers or drag our feet, more Americans will lose their jobs. More families will lose their savings. More dreams will be deferred and denied. And our nation will sink deeper into a crisis that, at some point, we may not be able to reverse.

That is not the country I know, and it is not a future I will accept as president of the United States. A world that depends on the strength of our economy is now watching and waiting for America to lead once more. And that is what we will do.

It will not come easy or happen overnight, and it is altogether likely that things may get worse before they get better. But that is all the more reason for Congress to act without delay. I know the scale of this plan is unprecedented, but so is the severity of our situation. We have already tried the wait-and-see approach to our problems, and it is the same approach that helped lead us to this day of reckoning.

That is why the time has come to build a 21st century economy in which hard work and responsibility are once again rewarded. That's why I'm asking Congress to work with me and my team day and night, on weekends if necessary, to get the plan passed in the next few weeks. That's why I'm calling on all Americans—Democrats and Republicans—to put good ideas ahead of the old ideological battles; a sense of common purpose above the same narrow partisanship; and insist that the first question each of us asks isn't "What's good for me?" but "What's good for the country my children will inherit?"

More than any program or policy, it is this spirit that will enable us to confront this challenge with the same spirit that has led previous generations to face down war, depression, and fear itself. And if we do—if we are able to summon that spirit again, if we are able to look out for one another, and listen to one another, and do our part for our nation and for posterity—then I have no doubt that years from now, we will look back on 2009 as one of those years that marked another new and hopeful beginning for the United States of America. Thank you, God Bless you, and may God Bless America.

Inaugural Address

U.S. CAPITOL, WASHINGTON, D.C.

JANUARY 20, 2009

Barack Obama

44TH PRESIDENT OF THE UNITED STATES OF AMERICA

My fellow citizens:

I stand here today humbled by the task before us, grateful for the trust you have bestowed, mindful of the sacrifices borne by our ancestors. I thank President Bush for his service to our nation, as well as the generosity and cooperation he has shown throughout this transition.

Forty-four Americans have now taken the presidential oath. The words have been spoken during rising tides of prosperity and the still waters of peace. Yet, every so often the oath is taken amidst gathering clouds and raging storms. At these moments, America has carried on not simply because of the skill or vision of those in high office, but because We the People have remained faithful to the ideals of our forbearers, and true to our founding documents.

> *" Today I say to you that the challenges we face are real. They are serious and they are many. They will not be met easily or in a short span of time. But know this, America—they will be met."*

So it has been. So it must be with this generation of Americans.

That we are in the midst of crisis is now well understood. Our nation is at war against a far-reaching network of violence and hatred. Our economy is badly weakened, a consequence of greed and irresponsibility on the part of some, but also our collective failure to make hard choices and prepare the nation for a new age. Homes have been lost; jobs shed; businesses shuttered. Our health care is too costly; our schools fail too many; and each day brings further evidence that the ways we use energy strengthen our adversaries and threaten our planet.

These are the indicators of crisis, subject to data and statistics. Less measurable but no less profound is a sapping of confidence across our land—a

> " We cannot help but believe that the old hatreds shall someday pass; that the lines of tribe shall soon dissolve; that as the world grows smaller, our common humanity shall reveal itself; and that America must play its role in ushering in a new era of peace. "

nagging fear that America's decline is inevitable, and that the next generation must lower its sights.

Today I say to you that the challenges we face are real. They are serious and they are many.

They will not be met easily or in a short span of time. But know this, America—they will be met. On this day, we gather because we have chosen hope over fear, unity of purpose over conflict and discord.

On this day, we come to proclaim an end to the petty grievances and false promises, the recriminations and worn-out dogmas, that for far too long have strangled our politics.

We remain a young nation, but in the words of Scripture, the time has come to set aside childish things. The time has come to reaffirm our enduring spirit; to choose our better history; to carry forward that precious gift, that noble idea, passed on from generation to generation: the God-given promise that all are equal, all are free, and all deserve a chance to pursue their full measure of happiness.

In reaffirming the greatness of our nation, we understand that greatness is never a given. It must be earned. Our journey has never been one of shortcuts or settling for less. It has not been the path for the fainthearted—for those who prefer leisure over work, or seek only the pleasures of riches and fame. Rather, it has been the risk-takers, the doers, the makers of things—some celebrated but more often men and women obscure in their labor—who have carried us up the long, rugged path towards prosperity and freedom.

For us, they packed up their few worldly possessions and traveled across oceans in search of a new life.

For us, they toiled in sweatshops and settled the West, endured the lash of the whip and plowed the hard earth.

For us, they fought and died, in places like Concord and Gettysburg, Normandy, and Khe Sahn. Time and again these men and women struggled and sacrificed and worked till their hands were raw so that we might live a better life. They saw America as bigger than the sum of our individual ambitions, greater than all the differences of birth or wealth or faction.

This is the journey we continue today. We remain the most prosperous, powerful nation on earth. Our workers are no less productive than when this crisis began. Our minds are no less inventive, our goods and services no less needed than they were last week or last month or last year. Our capacity remains undiminished. But our time of standing pat, of protecting narrow interests and putting off unpleasant decisions—that time has surely passed. Starting today, we must pick ourselves up, dust ourselves off, and begin again the work of remaking America.

For everywhere we look, there is work to be done. The state of the economy calls for action, bold and swift, and we will act—not only to create new jobs, but to lay a new foundation for growth. We will build the roads and bridges, the electric grids and digital lines, that feed our commerce and bind us together. We will restore science to its rightful place, and wield technology's wonders to raise health care's quality and lower its cost. We will harness the sun and the winds and the soil to fuel our cars and run our factories. And we will transform our schools and colleges and universities to meet the demands of a new age. All this we can do. And all this we will do.

Now, there are some who question the scale of our ambitions, who suggest that our system cannot tolerate too many big plans. Their memories are short. For they have forgotten what this country has already done, what free men and women can achieve when imagination is joined to common purpose, and necessity to courage.

What the cynics fail to understand is that the ground has shifted beneath them—that the stale political arguments that have consumed us for so long no longer apply. The question we ask today is not whether our government is too big or too small, but whether it works—whether it helps families find jobs at a decent wage, care they can afford, a retirement that is dignified. Where the answer is yes, we intend to move forward. Where the answer is no, programs will end. And those of us who manage the public's dollars will be held to account: to spend wisely, reform bad habits, and do our business in the light of day, because only then can we restore the vital trust between a people and their government.

Nor is the question before us whether the market is a force for good or ill. Its power to generate wealth and expand freedom is unmatched, but this crisis has reminded us that without a watchful eye, the market can spin out of control—and that a nation cannot prosper long when it favors only the prosperous. The success of our economy has always depended not just on the size of our gross domestic product, but on the reach of our prosperity, on our ability to extend opportunity to every willing heart—not out of charity, but because it is the surest route to our common good.

As for our common defense, we reject as false the choice between our safety and our ideals. Our Founding Fathers, faced with perils we can scarcely imagine, drafted a charter to assure the rule of law and the rights of man, a charter expanded by the blood of generations. Those ideals still light the world, and we will not give them up for expedience's sake. And so to all other peoples and governments who are watching today, from the grandest capitals to the small village where my father was born: know that America is a friend of each nation and every man, woman, and child who seeks a future of peace and dignity, and that we are ready to lead once more.

Recall that earlier generations faced down fascism and communism not just with missiles and tanks, but with sturdy alliances and enduring convictions. They understood that our power alone cannot protect us, nor does it entitle us to do as we please. Instead, they knew that our power grows through its prudent use, our security emanates from the justness of our cause, the force of our example, the tempering qualities of humility and restraint.

We are the keepers of this legacy. Guided by these principles once more, we can meet those new threats that demand even greater effort, even greater cooperation and understanding between nations. We will begin to responsibly leave Iraq to its people, and forge a hard-earned peace in Afghanistan. With old friends and former foes, we will work tirelessly to lessen the nuclear threat, and roll back the specter of a warming planet. We will not apologize for our way of life, nor will we waver in its defense, and for those who seek to advance their aims by inducing terror and slaughtering innocents, we say to you now that our spirit is stronger and cannot be broken, you cannot outlast us, and we will defeat you.

> *"What is required of us now is a new era of responsibility—a recognition, on the part of every American, that we have duties to ourselves, our nation, and the world, duties that we do not grudgingly accept but rather seize gladly."*

For we know that our patchwork heritage is a strength, not a weakness. We are a nation of Christians and Muslims, Jews and Hindus, and non-believers. We are shaped by every language and culture, drawn from every end of this earth, and because we have tasted the bitter swill of civil war and segregation, and emerged from that dark chapter stronger and more united, we cannot help but believe that the old hatreds shall someday pass; that the lines of tribe shall soon dissolve; that as the world grows smaller, our common humanity shall reveal itself; and that America must play its role in ushering in a new era of peace.

To the Muslim world, we seek a new way forward, based on mutual interest and mutual respect.

To those leaders around the globe who seek to sow conflict, or blame their society's ills on the West—know that your people will judge you on what you can build, not what you destroy. To those who cling to power through corruption and deceit and the silencing of dissent, know that you are on the wrong side of history, but that we will extend a hand if you are willing to unclench your fist.

To the people of poor nations, we pledge to work alongside you to make your farms flourish and let clean waters flow, to nourish starved bodies and feed hungry minds. And to those nations like ours that enjoy relative plenty, we say we can no longer afford indifference to suffering outside our borders; nor can we consume the world's resources without regard to effect. For the world has changed, and we must change with it.

As we consider the road that unfolds before us, we remember with humble gratitude those brave Americans who, at this very hour, patrol far-off deserts and distant mountains. They have something to tell us today, just as the fallen heroes who lie in Arlington whisper through the ages.

We honor them not only because they are guardians of our liberty, but because they embody the spirit of service: a willingness to find meaning in something greater than themselves. And yet, at this moment—a moment that will define a generation—it is precisely this spirit that must inhabit us all.

For as much as government can do and must do, it is ultimately the faith and determination of the American people upon which this nation relies. It is the kindness to take in a stranger when the levees break, the selflessness of workers who would rather cut their hours than see a friend lose their job, which sees us through our darkest hours. It is the firefighter's courage to storm a stairway filled with smoke, but also a parent's willingness to nurture a child, that finally decides our fate.

Our challenges may be new. The instruments with which we meet them may be new. But those values upon which our success depends—hard work and honesty, courage and fair play, tolerance and curiosity, loyalty and patriotism— these things are old. These things are true. They have been the quiet force of progress throughout our history. What is demanded then is a return to these truths. What is required of us now is a new era of responsibility—a recognition, on the part of every American, that we have duties to ourselves, our nation, and the world, duties that we do not grudgingly accept but rather seize gladly, firm in the knowledge that there is nothing so satisfying to the spirit, so defining of our character, than giving our all to a difficult task.

This is the price and the promise of citizenship.

This is the source of our confidence—the knowledge that God calls on us to shape an uncertain destiny.

This is the meaning of our liberty and our creed—why men and women and children of every race and every faith can join in celebration across this magnificent mall, and why a man whose father less than sixty years ago might not have been served at a local restaurant can now stand before you to take a most sacred oath.

> "With hope and virtue, let us brave once more the icy currents, and endure what storms may come. Let it be said by our children's children that when we were tested we refused to let this journey end, that we did not turn back nor did we falter."

So let us mark this day with remembrance, of who we are and how far we have traveled. In the year of America's birth, in the coldest of months, a small band of patriots huddled by dying campfires on the shores of an icy river. The capital was abandoned. The enemy was advancing. The snow was stained with blood. At a moment when the outcome of our revolution was most in doubt, the father of our nation ordered these words be read to the people:

"Let it be told to the future world...that in the depth of winter, when nothing but hope and virtue could survive...that the city and the country, alarmed at one common danger, came forth to meet [it]."

America, in the face of our common dangers, in this winter of our hardship, let us remember these timeless words. With hope and virtue, let us brave once more the icy currents, and endure what storms may come. Let it be said by our children's children that when we were tested, we refused to let this journey end, that we did not turn back nor did we falter; and with eyes fixed on the horizon and God's grace upon us, we carried forth that great gift of freedom and delivered it safely to future generations.